THE DARWEN COUNTY
HISTORY SERIES

A History of
SHROPSHIRE

A portion of the 1882 printing of the Ordnance Survey first edition One Inch to One Mile map, first published in 1833.

THE DARWEN COUNTY HISTORY SERIES

A History of
SHROPSHIRE

Barrie Trinder

Phillimore

1998

Published by
PHILLIMORE & CO. LTD.
Shopwyke Manor Barn, Chichester, West Sussex

First published 1983
Second edition 1998

ISBN 1 86077 036 3

Printed and bound in Great Britain by
BUTLER AND TANNER LTD.
London and Frome

Contents

List of Illustrations

Frontispiece : Shrewsbury in 1882

List of Colour Illustrations

Preface and Acknowledgements

It is gratifying that the first edition of this work has been out of print for several years, and that the publishers wish to include Shropshire amongst the first county histories to be produced in the new format for the series. I have retained the basic structure of the book, but have taken the opportunity to correct some errors and misprints, and to revise some sections where recent scholarship has added to or amended our understanding of Shropshire's past.

A work of synthesis of this kind depends on the labours of many other people, and I would like to express my thanks to the following students, friends and colleagues on whose work I have drawn: Poppy Anderson, Andrew Arroll, Philip Barker, the late Norah Barnett, George Baugh, Sarah Beard, Paul Beck, David Bilbey, Ivor Brown, Ian Burrow, Joyce Butt, Martin Carver, Bill Champion, the late Robin Chaplin, Janice Cox, Nancy and Jeff Cox, Connie Evason, the late Roy Fletcher, Peter Forsaith, the late George Foxall, Philippa Gray, Tony Herbert, Peter Hewitt, David Hey, Liz Hinkley, Andrew Jenkinson, Peter Klein, Ian Lawley, Madge Moran, Sam Mullins, the late Norman Mutton, Jonathan Nichol, David Pannett, the late John Pilgrim, the late Bill Pollard, Fred Powell, John Powell, Derrick Pratt, Janet and Olive Richards, Norman Rowley, Trevor Rowley, Patricia Sibcey, Alan Snell, Martin Speight, Stanley Stanford, Michael Stratton, Julian Temple, Emyr Thomas, Peter Toghill, Geoffrey Toms, the late Gordon Tucker, Rosemary Tudge, Margot Usher, Malcolm Wanklyn, Graham Webster and Michael Wise. I am indebted to Tony Carr, Marion Roberts, James Lawson, David Lloyd and Richard Morgan, who read the text of the first edition, made many useful suggestions and saved me from some embarrassing errors. Any mistakes or misjudgements which remain are entirely my responsibility.

I would also like thank the staff of the Shropshire Local Studies Library for their cheerful and informed assistance, and to Janet Markland and Carol Sampson of the Ironbridge Institute for help with the production of the text.

I am also grateful to Shirley Reynolds and to Pat Read who provided the illustrations for the first edition.

As always I am grateful to my wife and daughter for their company, comments and forbearance.

BARRIE TRINDER

1

Definitions

Most of my generation who grew up in the south or the Midlands first knew Shropshire as somewhere to be passed through on the way to Wales, a successions of traffic hold-ups between Birmingham and Rhyl, a late-opening fish-and-chip shop half-way from Oxford to Llanberis or Boston Lodge, or the Wrekin emerging through the mists of a summer dawn as a Castle class 4-6-0 headed westwards from Wellington on the Midnight from Paddington. In the 1950s, to a young outsider, Shropshire's history amounted to a few castles designed to keep out the Welsh, several not especially luxurious youth hostels, and some cosy market-town teashops. The significance of the county's past was scarcely recognised beyond its own boundaries.

Shropshire is unmistakably a border county. It has many Welsh place names, and Welsh is still spoken in the streets, cafés, chapels and choral societies of Shrewsbury and Oswestry. Few English counties were defended by so many castles. Yet Shropshire's history is more than border warfare.

1 *The western ramparts of the Iron-Age hillfort of Old Oswestry (SJ294310).*

It is a history of highlanders and lowlanders meeting over many centuries in the market place as well as on the battlefield. It encompasses centuries of sheep farming and whimberry gathering on wildly beautiful hillsides, and the manufacture of some of the world's best cheese from the milk of placid herds grazing on the beds of reclaimed meres. Such herds were disturbed by Parliamentary and Royalist cavalry in the 1640s and by new Spitfires under test three centuries later. It is a history of landed gentlemen riding from their ancestral homes to sit at Quarter Sessions, to discuss agricultural improvements, turnpike roads and new canals, to choose MPs, to exchange geological specimens, to gossip about their neighbours' wives, to set up regiments and to subscribe to hospitals. It is also a history of mining and manufacturing, of technological innovations which in the last 250 years have helped to bring about dramatic changes in the life of the whole western world, changes which were stimulated by the ambitions of entrepreneurs, both Salopians and immigrants, and made possible by six-year-old boys regulating the ventilation of mines, and by teenage girls picking iron ore on pit banks.

Shropshire has inherited a rich legacy of antiquarian scholarship. The Rev. R.W. Eyton's *Antiquities of Shropshire* answers questions about every parish in the county which would take years of research to uncover. Dean Cranage's *Shropshire Churches* is similarly comprehensive, while over a century of research is recorded in the transactions of the county's archaeological society. Richard Gough's *History of Myddle*, written about 1700, is not just the first parish history, but a richly-detailed portrayal of provincial

2 Offa's Dyke to the south of the River Ceiriog in the far north-western corner of Shropshire (SJ261372), showing the deep ditch on the Welsh side and the bank on the English side which was originally between three and four metres high. This stretch of the dyke forms the boundary between Shropshire and Wales.

life in the 17th century. During the last 30 years there has been an explosion of popular interest in the history of Shropshire, expressed in new museums, the work of civic societies, the publication of popular guidebooks, the opening to the public of old buildings and the designation of long-distance foot-paths. Few people with any interest in the English past have not now heard of Ironbridge, one of the cradles of the Industrial Revolution, of Ludlow, the archetypal planned town, or of the Offa's Dyke Footpath. The county's history is no longer unrecognised.

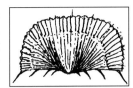

3 *Protocenites Ludloviensis.*

Shropshire came into existence as a unit of government in the early 10th century. During the middle ages its extent varied as large areas fell under the rule of the Marcher lords, and were lost to the jurisdiction of the sheriff. The county took its present form, subject to minor variations, in the reign of Henry VIII, when the Marcher lordships were abolished, and the Welsh counties defined. Part of Halesowen was linked to Shropshire from the late 11th century, and remained a detached portion of the county until it was returned to Worcestershire in 1844. At the same time, Farlow, an enclave of Herefordshire, became part of Shropshire, by which it was entirely surrounded. Farlow was in Shropshire in Domesday Book, but had pre-Conquest links with Leominster, and soon after 1086 was regarded as part of Herefordshire. Further minor alterations to the boundary were made in 1895, 1936 and 1965.

The oldest known form of the name of the county is SCROBBESCIRE, the shire belonging to SCROBBESBYRIG, the Saxon name for Shrews-bury. After the Norman Conquest the county's new rulers adopted the forms SALOPESCIRE and SALOPESBIRY. The word SALOP, applying both to the county and the county town, survived from the middle ages as an alternative English form, having originally been abbreviated from the Norman French. A Latin form, SALOPIA, was commonly used in documents in the 16th century, and in subsequent centuries legal records refer to the County of Salop rather than to Shropshire. The new authority established in 1974 under the Local Government Act of 1972 was officially named Salop, but this was altered to Shropshire with effect from 1 March 1980.

Shropshire's history has been shaped by its varied geology. Rocks from 10 of the 12 recognised geological periods can be found in Shropshire. Many of the county's most distinctive peaks, the Wrekin, the Lawley, Caer Caradoc and Earl's Hill among them, date from the pre-Cambrian period, between 900 and 570 million years ago, and are formed of volcanic ashes and lavas. The Wrekin was never, as is sometimes supposed, a volcano, nor is it the highest point in England, as was commonly believed when Celia Fiennes visited Shropshire in 1698, nor even the highest point in Shropshire, since its height of 1,334 feet is comfortably exceeded by the summits of Brown Clee (1,772 feet), the Stiperstones (1,762 feet), Titterstone Clee (1,750 feet), the Long Mynd (1,695 feet) and Caer Caradoc (1,506 feet). During the Cambrian, Ordovician and Silurian periods, between 570 and 400 million years ago, when Shropshire lay almost continuously under the sea, Wenlock Edge, Clun Forest, the limestones around Ludlow and the mineral-rich area

4 *Earthworks which conceal the remains of the castle and town built by the Corbets, one of the principal families of Marcher lords, at Caus (SJ336078) in the 12th and 13th centuries.*

around the Stiperstones were formed. From the Devonian period come the Old Red Sandstones of the Corvedale and Clee Hills region, and from the Carboniferous period, between 350 and 180 million years ago, the coalfields of Coalbrookdale, Wyre Forest and Shrewsbury, and the limestone belt which stretches northwards from Llanymynech Hill. The sandstones of the North Shropshire plain and of the area east of the Severn around Bridgnorth were laid down in the Parmian and Triassic periods between 280 and 190 million years ago. The clays, sands and gravels which cover much of the North Shropshire plain were deposited by the sheets of ice which covered much of the county about two million years ago. When this ice melted the River Severn, which had previously run into the Dee, overflowed to the east and cut the passage through the Carboniferous and Silurian rocks which is now called the Ironbridge Gorge. The meres and mosses of North Shropshire, and the whole hummocky landscape which extends from just south of Shrewsbury to the Cheshire border, are also legacies of the Ice Age.

Shropshire's geology is of more than local significance, for the county was studied by several pioneers of the science, among them Adam Sedgwick and Sir Roderick Murchison. Many standard geological features are named after the Shropshire locations where they were first observed. Uriconian and Long Myndian rocks are recognised in all parts of the world, as are fossils like Protocenites Ludloviensis or Lunata Salopina.

Salopians living in the Black Park north of Whitchurch, or fifty miles to the south on the banks of the Teme at Burford, would accept that their heritage includes Robert Clive, Charles Darwin, the *Feathers* at Ludlow, the Old Work at Wroxeter and the Iron Bridge in a way that those of their Cheshire and Worcestershire neighbours do not. This is the justification for a county history, a study of those activities in which its people have come together and a framework for understanding the history of the many and diverse communities of which Shropshire is made up.

2

From the Mists of Prehistory

The earliest remains of Man's activities in the area now called Shropshire are scrapers and other implements made from local pebble flint, found chiefly in such parishes as Worfield, Claverley and Alveley along the county's south-eastern border. These implements date from the Mesolithic or Middle Stone Age, about 4000 B.C. Any evidence of the activities of the men of the earlier Palaeolithic period was probably destroyed when glaciers eroded the levels in which it rested. From the later Neolithic period there remain an arrowhead found on the Wrekin, and several stone axes, some made from stone from as far away as Cornwall and Charnwood Forest.

By 2000 B.C. there were settled communities in most parts of Britain, and there is plentiful evidence in Shropshire of the people of this Bronze-Age civilisation. Some 25 burial mounds survive on the Long Mynd, most of them along the line of the ancient track known as the Port Way. Bronze-Age burials have been found on the gravel terrace south of Shrewsbury. The plain north of Ludlow is particularly rich in remains of this period. Dr Stanley Stanford has shown that the area he calls the Bromfield Necropolis was used for burials for about eight centuries from approximately 1550 B.C. Mitchell's Fold and the Hoarstones, the stone circles on the county's western border, served some kind of ritual or astronomical purpose for the people of this period, who probably also made the dug-out canoes found in such marshy places as the meres, the Perry valley and Marton Pool. Evidence of arable cultivation and of enclosures connected with the stock farming of this period can be seen on the Shropshire hills. The late Miss Lily Chitty showed from the evidence of flints collected from

5 *Mitchell's Fold stone circle near Stapely Hill (SO304984) which is probably of Bronze-Age date. It is between 26 and 27.4 m. in diameter, and consists of some 14 or 15 standing stones.*

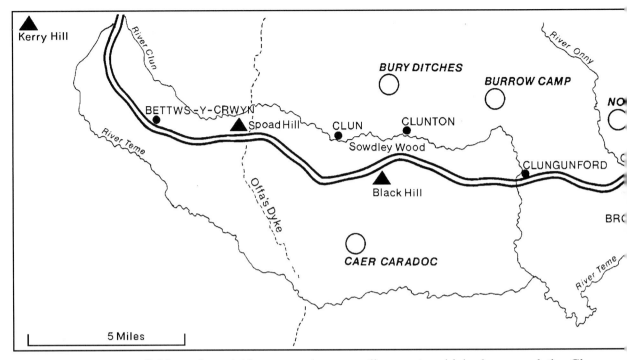

6 *The Clee-Clun Ridgeway.*

fields and roadside verges that a trading route which she named the Clee-Clun Ridgeway extended across South Shropshire from Kerry Hill to a Severn crossing near Bewdley. Along it were brought into the region flints from the Marlborough Downs or East Anglia, while stone axes made at Hyssington near Corndon Hill were exported.

The outstanding monuments of prehistoric man in Shropshire are the county's 25 or so hillforts. Evidence of Bronze-Age origins has been discovered on several of them, but they are essentially the creation of the Iron-Age civilisation established in the region from about 800 B.C. The phrase 'hill top towns' perhaps describes their functions better than 'hillforts'. In recent decades excavators have shown that every hillfort within the region which has been investigated was permanently occupied. Within the deep ditches and high, stockade-topped ramparts of these settlements were closely packed rectangular and round huts, some used for accommodation and some for storage. Dr Stanford has suggested that they could have supported as many as 210 people per hectare, which means that the population of a fort like the Wrekin could have been in the region of a thousand.

Evidence has been accumulating in recent decades of the lowland settlements of the Iron-Age peoples. Traces of many farmsteads have been discovered by aerial photography, particularly along the Severn Valley between Montford Bridge and Buildwas. One group of sites at Weeping Cross (or Sharpstones Hill), on the edge of Shrewsbury was excavated in the late 1960s in advance of housing development. The archaeologists revealed foundations of round Iron-Age huts within rectangular enclosures bounded by earthen ramparts and ditches, all of which overlay Bronze-Age burial mounds.

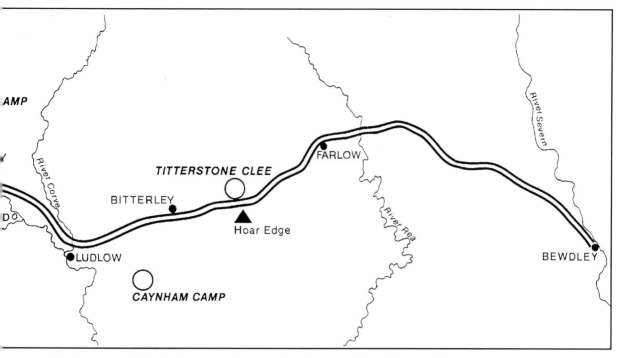

By the year A.D. 1 it seems that much of present-day Shropshire was governed from the hillfort on the Wrekin, the centre of administration of the tribe known to the Romans as the Cornovii. Some time before A.D. 50 the Roman armies, which had landed in the south-east in A.D. 43, arrived in the West Midlands. Aerial photography has revealed a temporary Roman military camp near Eye Farm, Leighton, with a characteristic rectangular plan with rounded corners. About A.D. 48 the Romans forced the British prince Caratacus into submission, in a campaign which was probably based on a fortified camp at Wroxeter. The sparse description by Tacitus of Caratacus's last stand has led antiquarians to speculate inconclusively about its location. In A.D. 57 there was an attempt to subjugate the whole of present-day Wales, and it was probably at this time that the 14th Legion moved its headquarters from Mancetter on Watling Street to Wroxeter. There is evidence from other parts of the county of Roman military activities in the first century A.D. At Wall near Cleobury Mortimer is a square enclosure some 1.8 hectares in extent, which excavations in 1960-61 established to have been a Roman military settlement. Buildings of the military period have been identified at Whitchurch (or Mediolanum), and in the far north of the county a large camp, some 19.37 hectares in extent, has been identified on the banks of the Ceiriog at Rhyn Park.

By the year A.D. 80 Chester had become a more logical site than Wroxeter for the principal military base in the region. The fortress at Wroxeter was carefully demolished about A.D. 90. The site of the military encampment became a civilian settlement, the tribal capital of the Cornovii, and one of the more remote outposts of Roman civilisation.

3

Roman and British Rule

The Romans began to develop Wroxeter as a centre of civilian government towards the end of the first century A.D. It has been suggested that the 20th Legion may have been constructing a group of baths buildings as a gift to the town at the time they were summoned northwards. The baths were never completed, and the construction of the city seems initially to have proceeded slowly, but it was accelerated in the third decade of the second century, perhaps as a result of a visit by the Emperor Hadrian in A.D. 122. The inscription on the front of the forum identified Wroxeter as the *Civitas Cornoviorum*, the seat of government of the Cornovii.

When defences were constructed around Wroxeter at the end of the second century A.D. they enclosed an area of 63 hectares and consisted of a 4-km double rampart, topped by a palisaded stockade. The city was supplied with water by an aqueduct, 1.2km long, which was fed by the Bell Brook. The forum which measures 74m x 21m is large in comparison with others in Roman Britain. The Old Work, the wall which still stands, was part of the Palaestra or Baths Basilica, the exercise hall of the bath house, which measured 73m x 69m. Bronze busts and brooches were made by the lost wax process by some of the many metal-working craftsmen who flourished in the city. Some time between 165 and 185 there was a fire which caused a panic during which many market stalls were knocked over. One of them belonged to a seller of Samian pottery, who obtained supplies from manufacturers at Lezoux near Clermont Ferrand and Reinzabern in the Rhineland. Wroxeter's more important buildings had ceilings with ornate

7 *The inscription commemorating the dedication of the forum at Wroxeter during the reign of the Emperor Hadrian in A.D. 133.*

20

plaster vaulting and floors of mosaic and herring-bone tiles. Doors were
secured by locks and padlocks. Citizens used such tools as pruning hooks,
meat choppers and claw-footed wrenches, wrote with pens or styli, and
gambled with ornate gaming pieces.

8 *The Old Work at
Wroxeter (SJ565088)
which was part of the*
Palaestra *or Basilica, the
exercise hall of the
public baths.*

   Evidence of Roman civilisation outside Wroxeter is less plentiful. The
network of roads in the county has been mapped and some military sites
have been identified. Eight possible villa sites have been identified, some of
which have produced mosaic floors, but not all were certainly large houses.
Many farmstead sites have been identified by aerial photography. The
Romans certainly used the metallic ores in Shropshire. Five pigs of lead
bearing inscriptions naming the Emperor Hadrian have been found near
the Stiperstones, and a hoard of 30 Roman denarii was discovered in 1965
in the copper mine or *Ogof* on Llanymynech Hill. Aerial reconnaissance has
revealed remains of Roman prospecting at Linley, where there was probably
no ore.

   Understanding of the period which followed the end of Roman rule
suffers from the encrustation of centuries of myth-making, but developments on several fronts during the last two decades are destroying many of

9 *The north wall of St Andrew's Church, Wroxeter (SJ564083). An archaeological survey has suggested that the wall dates from the seventh or the eighth century AD. Much of it consists of re-used masonry from the Roman city, and a small shaft, placed on edge, can be observed between the two medieval windows.*

10 *Crop marks at Atcham (SJ552115) photographed in 1975. The two rectangular features to the left of the road, by the small tree, have been interpreted as a Dark-Age settlement, possibly an aisled hall palace similar to that at Yeavering, Northumberland, which dates from the early seventh century. The curving features to the right of the road indicate the partially ploughed-out course of the Shrewsbury Canal, opened in 1797.*

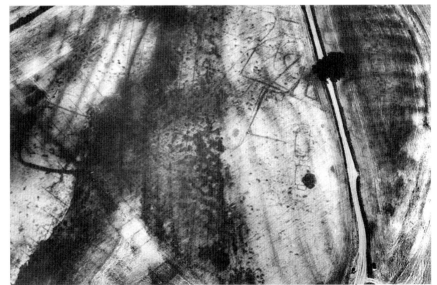

11 *The Berth at Baschurch (SJ429236), a fortified site sur-rounded by marshes which has been suggested as a possible seat of authority in the central part of Shropshire in the sixth and seventh centuries.*

the fabrications of previous generations. Philip Barker's excavations on the site of the Baths Basilica at Wroxeter show that settlement continued there well into the fifth century. Excavations at several hillforts have produced evidence that they were re-occupied in the post-Roman period. At Bromfield, Dr. Stanley Stanford has found an early, apparently immediately post-pagan Saxon cemetery. The work of Dr. John Morris shows that the Welsh poems of the period, however corrupted in later centuries, contain sound historical evidence.

Whatever the uncertainties about the post-Roman period, it seems that it was a time of economic as well as political crisis, of declining population, which was not matched by the inflow of new migrations. Bubonic plague ravaged the whole of Western Europe in the years around A.D. 550. Settlements seem to have been relatively transient, and areas which had once been cultivated reverted to waste.

By the early fourth century the public buildings of Wroxeter were falling out of use but the commercial life of the city continued. Excavations in the Macellum have revealed many coins of the house of Valentian from between A.D. 364 and 383.

During the fourth century Roman troops were sent from Britain to resist barbarian pressures on the Rhine and the Danube. In 410, the year when the Goths took Rome, the Emperor Honorius declined responsibility for the defence of Britain, and after about 420 the money-based economy collapsed. For more than 200 years afterwards Shropshire was ruled by the princes of the Cornovii.

In Britain as a whole in the early fifth century barbarian raiders were dispersed, but the local rulers turned on each other in civil war. Saxon mercenaries were brought in from the Continent, who ultimately turned against the various British factions. From about 460 resistance stiffened under Ambrosius Aurelianus and the native rulers re-established their supremacy at the battle of Badon in the late fifth century. By about 460 the territory of the Coritani, the tribe based on Leicester and Lincoln, had been occupied by Saxon invaders, who had been halted roughly along the line of Watling Street, to the east of the Shropshire border. Cunorix, 'son of the son of the holly', an Irishman whose tomb, dating from between 460 and 480 has been found at Wroxeter, probably belonged to a group of mercenaries employed in the warfare of this period.

In the early seventh century the rulers of present-day Shropshire faced increasing pressure from the Saxon kingdom of Mercia, whose capital was Tamworth. At the same time they had many contacts with the Angles who controlled the kingdom of Northumbria. In 642 Oswald of Northumbria was killed in a battle at Oswestry with a Mercian army led by King Penda. In 655 Penda himself was killed, and for a time Oswiu, brother of Oswald, reduced the power of the Mercians, but by 658 Penda's son Wulfhere had established Mercian supremacy in the region.

The evidence of Welsh poems suggests that the Cornovii remained independent in the lifetime of Penda. Their territory had probably been partitioned. In the second decade of the seventh century a prince called

12 *Mosaic from the Roman villa at Yarchester near Much Wenlock, discovered in 1957.*

Cyndrwyn ruled in the area around Wroxeter, while one Constantine governed from Kenchester in Herefordshire, and the division between their territories was probably perpetuated in the ancient boundaries between the dioceses of Lichfield and Hereford. The career of Cynddylan, son of the Cyndrwyn who fought in the Battle of Chester, was celebrated by a bard who looked across Shropshire from the Wrekin. He suggested that Cynddylan refused to pay tribute to a Saxon king about the year 655, and subsequently won a victory against a Saxon army at Wall near Lichfield. Soon afterwards he was killed, probably in a skirmish with Oswiu and a Northumbrian army, in 656. His sons fled to Powys, and Shropshire passed under the control of the Mercian kings at Tamworth. Some authorities would argue that war was not a significant factor and that the people of what is now Shropshire joined Mercia voluntarily, but the evidence for the extension of Mercian authority in the mid-seventh century, by whatever means, seems well established. The people of the region, the Wreocensetan, were listed in the Tribal Hidage, a census of Mercian territories drawn up about 661, and Wulfhere's Ford, near Melverley, is perhaps the site of a treaty made between the Mercian king and the rulers of Powys.

Archaeological evidence does not conflict with that of the Welsh poems. It has been shown that after the baths at Wroxeter were abandoned about 300 the roof and other parts of the building were systematically demolished. Flimsy timber buildings were erected amidst the ruins, but about 450 they were cleared away and hundreds of tons of finely sifted rubble were laid as a foundation for two series of large timber-framed two-storey buildings. The buildings seem to have been of classical proportions, with at least two storeys, and porticoes in the classical style, suggesting that the rulers of Wroxeter in this period had inherited much from Roman civilisation. The remains have some affinities with those of large-scale Roman villas, and may indicate that an individual leader had taken over as his private property what had previously been a prime public site. The tomb of Cunorix shows that the central part of Wroxeter was occupied in the late fifth century, and the identification of at least five phases of building after the early fourth century makes it possible that occupation continued until after 500. It seems likely that the area around the Forum and the Baths Basilica was abandoned during the sixth century, but it was neither burned by rampaging Saxons nor did it collapse in poverty. Its timber buildings were demolished and its inhabitants apparently moved elsewhere. In a time of declining population it may have become indefensible. Recent research has suggested that the north wall of the present parish church of St Andrew, Wroxeter is a fragment of a building of seventh- or eighth-century date, and it is possible that the inhabitants of the city may have congregated in its south-western corner near the river crossing where the church now stands when the central area became private property. The church could have been constructed from fragments of Roman masonry after the occupation by the newly-Christian kings of Mercia.

It seems credible that the rulers of the lowland Cornovii transferred their seat of government away from Wroxeter. They may have moved to

Shrewsbury, but the earliest mention of the town in a document is as late as 901, and archaeological evidence cannot date settlement on the site before the eighth century. The new seat of government could have been the Wrekin hillfort. It could have been The Berth, north of Baschurch, a fortification on a low hilltop, surrounded by marshes, where a bronze cauldron dating from the seventh century has been found. One Welsh poem relates that Cynddylan was killed in battle and taken to the churches of Bassa, which would certainly accord with the use of The Berth as a seat of government. Another possible site is the ford on the Severn at Atcham, adjacent to the church dedicated to the seventh-century Northumbrian bishop St Eata. Aerial reconnaissance in Atcham parish in 1975 revealed cropmarks indicating buildings of approximate size 14m x 8m, and 24m x 8 m, which were probably aisled. The larger building is similar to the great hall at Yeavering, the palace in Northumberland which was built by King Aethelfrith, and remained in use until the time of Oswiu, whose Mercian contemporary Wulfhere brought an end to British rule over the Wrocansaetan. It is one of many links between Shropshire and Northumbria which require further elucidation.

The original dedication of the parish church of Cressage to St Samson suggests that Christianity may have continued in Shropshire from the end of Roman rule until the establishment of Mercian authority in the seventh century. St Samson was born in Wales and travelled widely during the sixth century. Many churches in Cornwall and Brittany bear his name, and are usually in places which he visited. His biographer relates that early in his itinerant life he set up a church by a great river near a Roman camp, and it seems likely that he was for a time at Cressage. No pagan Saxon burials have yet been found in Shropshire, although graves excavated at Bromfield seem to be of the early Christian period. The inclusion of knives suggests that those who were buried there were recently converted Saxons. The Mercians adopted Roman Christianity in the time of Wulfhere and, if the Cornovii had retained their Christianity, the lack of pagan graves in Shropshire would be explicable.

Shropshire's place names provide evidence of the extent of Mercian authority. In most parts of the county Saxon names predominate. There are many places whose names are compounds of the Saxon word '-tun': ten Astons, eight Westons, eight Suttons, eight Actons, seven Nortons, six Eatons, five Uptons, five Prestons and five Eytons.

The period from 350 to 650 is the most confused in the history of Shropshire. New interpretations of documentary sources and archaeological excavations may expand our understanding, but just as important as new evidence is the apt use of terms. The period should not be interpreted as a long transition from one form of alien rule to another, nor just as the decline of Wroxeter and the establishment of a new seat of authority. For between 200 and 300 years after the time that the region ceased effectively to be ruled from Rome, it was governed by native British rulers. This was no mere passing phase but a distinct period in the county's history, scarcely shorter than the period of rule from Rome.

13 *The north wall of the church of St Andrew, Wroxeter, which incorporates Roman masonry, including what appears to be a small column set on edge. The wall is now considered to date from either the seventh or eighth century.*

4

The County Established

During the 650s the area now called Shropshire became subject to the recently Christianised Mercian kings ruling from Tamworth. Some time before 690 the Mercian royal house established the monastery of St Milburga at Much Wenlock, endowing it with properties in south Shropshire. St Milburga was the daughter of Merewald, third son of King Penda who had been made sub-king of the Magonsaete, the British tribe who lived in Herefordshire and south Shropshire. She was related to Ethelred and Coelred, who died respectively in 704 and 716, both of whom ruled as kings of Mercia. St Milburga herself ruled the abbey from the time of its foundation or shortly afterwards. Like other contemporary religious houses, the community was a double monastery, consisting of both monks and nuns, who appear to have worshipped in separate churches. Excavations have suggested that Roman buildings on the site of the late Cluniac Priory were reoccupied when the double monastery was established. The women's order disappeared, but it seems that the order of monks evolved into a community of priests serving a minster church.

The Mercians built Wats Dyke which extends from the Dee estuary to Pentre-coed on the Morda Brook south of Oswestry. Some nine miles of the dyke, stretching southwards from the point where it crosses the River Ceiriog, are in Shropshire. The dyke was probably constructed as a boundary in the late seventh century.

Wats Dyke pales into insignificance by comparison with the boundary erected between the English and the Welsh by Offa, who ruled Mercia between 757 and 796. Offa was a figure of European significance, who dealt on equal terms with Charlemagne. The dyke extends over a hundred miles from the estuary of the Wye to the mouth of the Dee. Some of its most impressive sections are in Shropshire, including the breathtaking ascent southwards out of the Ceiriog Valley, and the magnificent stretches on the heights of Clun Forest, and it forms three lengths of the county boundary.

The surveys of Sir Cyril Fox in the 1920s and '30s established that Offa's Dyke incorporates almost all the most fertile lowland territory in England, and was obviously constructed at a time when Mercian power was predominant. Recent excavations on the sites of what Fox thought were original 'gaps' have shown that the dyke was actually continuous at these points. Contrary to Fox's suppositions, the dyke may have been a defensive frontier, manned at regular intervals. The dyke consists of a western

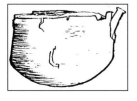

14 *A seventh-century cauldron found at The Berth, Baschurch.*

26

ditch and a bank which may once have been three or four metres high. It is a formidable fortification, which must rank as one of the most impressive memorials in Europe to the authority of the monarchs of the Dark Ages.

During the first two centuries of Mercian rule the town of Shrewsbury came into existence. A document of 901 records a transaction made 'in civitate Scrobbensis'. The Latin word *civitas* implies a place from which authority was exercised over a wide area, and the status of the town is indicated by the establishment of a mint there by the 920s. *Scrobbensis* is probably a Latin form of the word *Scrobbesbyrig* used in a document a century later, the latter syllables of which suggest a fortified place. The name has been interpreted as an eminence covered with shrubs, but more recently the view that the *Scrob* element refers to a personal name has gained support. The only archaeological evidence which throws any light on the origins of Shrewsbury is a five-inch long 'pin', possibly used for dressing hair, or perhaps as a stylus, which was found on the site of Old St Chad's church in 1889. It dates from the eighth or ninth century, and is the earliest unequivocal evidence for Saxon settlement. The archaeological evidence on its own is insufficient to indicate even the existence of a Saxon *town* on the site. Like other towns which originated in the Saxon period, Stafford, Bristol, Oxford and Worcester, Shrewsbury stood on a promontory largely surrounded by marshes, and it is possible that the boggy ground bordering the river rather than walls or ditches formed the town's defences. Shrewsbury stands on the boundary between the dioceses of Lichfield and Hereford, which probably represents the border between the post-Roman peoples of the Wreocensetan, whose centre had once been Wroxeter, and the Magonsaetan, who occupied what is now south Shropshire and Herefordshire. It is doubtful whether a seat of government would have been established

15 *A lane at Weston (SJ300280) near Oswestry which follows the course of Wats Dyke. While the dyke can be traced across Shropshire for about nine miles, its remains are nowhere comparable with those of Offa's Dyke.*

16 *The eighth- or ninth-century pin or stylus found on the site of old St Chad's church, Shrewsbury.*

on such a frontier before the two peoples acknowledged the same authority, which suggests a mid- or late rather than an early Saxon date for the foundation of Shrewsbury.

The Saxon shire which took its name from *Scrobbesbyrig* came into existence, along with other West Midlands shires, in the early 10th century, probably during a reorganisation of government in response to pressure from Scandinavian armies. Most of the Mercian shires are of 1,200 hides or multiples of 1,200. (A hide was a unit of taxation, the meaning of which has been much debated.) The shire was made up of the territory of the Wreocensetan, and sufficient of the area of the Magonsaetan to make up 2,400 hides. The remaining 1,500 hides of the Magonsaetan became a shire governed from Hereford.

The power of the Mercian kings was destroyed by invaders from Scandinavia who first descended on England in 793. After many raids of increasing ferocity in the first half of the ninth century, a substantial army arrived in East Anglia in 865. In 874 they forced King Burgred of Mercia to flee to Rome, and set up their own nominee King Ceolwulf II in his place. Ceolwulf died, the last king of Mercia, about 886, after which those parts of his kingdom which were not ruled by the Danes, including Shropshire, came under the influence of the kings of Wessex. In 893 Danes built an encampment at Quatford. Danish power was gradually reduced by Edward, son of Alfred, and by his sister Aethelflaed, widow of Aethelred, ealdorman of Mercia. Aethelflaed built 10 *burghs* or fortresses in the Midlands to resist the Danes, one of which was completed at Quatford. Shropshire was involved with the renewed struggles against the Scandinavians in the early 11th century and the entry in the Anglo-Saxon Chronicle for the year 1006 recording that King Ethelred the Unready had 'gone across the Thames into Shropshire and received there his food-rents in the Christmas season' is the first documentary reference to the county.

The system of administration in Shropshire became more elaborate during the early 11th century. The *hundreds*, ancient divisions of land which pre-dated the formation of the shire, seem to have been modified. The duties of the sheriff, who acted in the shire for the king, were defined. Much of Shropshire was laid waste by the Welsh in the years before the Norman Conquest of 1066, and recovery took several decades. The county revealed by Domesday Book, compiled in 1086, differs in several respects from the modern Shropshire. The area around Montgomery then belonged to Shropshire, as did the hundred of Wigmore in present-day Herefordshire. Much of Clun Forest was under Welsh rule, and several parishes east of the Severn downstream from Bridgnorth, including Worfield, Claverley and Alveley, were in Staffordshire. Domesday Book is the first documentary record of the majority of present-day settlements in the county, and must be the starting point for any serious investigation of the history of a parish. A large part of Shropshire was held under the king by Roger de Montgomery, one of the few followers of William I with the rank of earl. Domesday Book suggests that the most valuable lands in the county were those around Shrewsbury and in the Corvedale. Much of North Shropshire was relatively poor, partly as the result of recent warfare.

5

The Open Fields and After

Most of the Shropshire parishes mentioned in Domesday Book contained several townships or hamlets. Dawley, for example, consisted of the townships of Dawley Magna, Dawley Parva and Malins Lee. Larger parishes, many of which were situated along the Welsh border, contained many townships. The name Ruyton-XI-Towns reveals how many hamlets there were in the parish in the middle ages. Each township had its group of two, three or four open fields which were cultivated in common by the peasants, each tenant having several strips scattered about each of the fields. Evidence of open-field cultivation can be found in most townships in the county. The *Victoria County History* demonstrated conclusively that every hamlet in the hundreds of Ford and Condover had its own open fields. The three fields in the township of Wrockwardine were still being cultivated in 1674 when they were called the Dale, Killstone and Wide fields. Clee St Margaret's arable land in 1623 consisted of the Stanley, Frith and Oxley fields. Samuel Garbet in his *History of Wem* written in the mid-18th century names the open fields of most of the townships in the parish.

17 *The valley which descends from Monkey's Fold, the shoulder between Abdon Burf and Clee Burf on Brown Clee Hill (SO597853). The stream in the valley forms the boundary between the parish of Abdon to the left and Clee St Margaret to the right. Alongside it ran a straker route, by which tenants could take their beasts to the common pasture on top of the hill. On the Abdon side of the boundary the fields were created at the time of parliamentary enclosure early in the 19th century. The fields which extend into the waste land on the Clee St Margaret side were made by squatters in the settlement of Cockshutford.*

The existence of open fields is indicated by many field name elements, like *ridges, lands, reans* (i.e. the drainage furrows), *furlongs* (the units in which strips were arranged), *shuts, headlands, butts,* or *yards* (i.e. yardlands, or groups of furrows). Field evidence of open-field cultivation, which usually takes the form of ridge and furrow, the corrugated surfaces created by mould board ploughs, is less common in Shropshire than in some other Midland counties, but small portions can be observed in many parishes. Some of the best preserved ridge and furrow surrounds the deserted hamlet of Lawton in Diddlebury parish in the Corvedale.

The open-field system was in existence in the Borderland by the time of the Norman Conquest. Excavations near the castle at Hen Domen, Montgomery, which was in Shropshire in the 11th century, have shown that there was ridge and furrow on the site before the Normans built the castle, and research in High Ercall has suggested that the peasant holdings in the open fields pre-dated the Conquest. The only part of Shropshire where there were no open fields was the north-western corner near Oswestry, where the original pattern of settlement seems to have consisted of isolated farmsteads rather than nucleated townships. Large parts of Shropshire appear not to have been cultivated in the middle ages, uplands like the Long Mynd and Clun Forest, wetlands like the Weald Moors, Whixall Moss and the Boggy Moors, and sandy heaths like Northwood Common and Hind Heath, but by 1086 such areas were mostly attached to particular townships and used for grazing or as sources of wood or peat.

The *Victoria County History* has shown that in the hundreds of Ford and Condover about 1200 the area of open field attached to each township remained relatively small 'islands' surrounded by extensive stretches of woodland and moor. Such areas were gradually brought into cultivation by *assarting* or clearance, which is often reflected in names like *stockings* (land covered with stumps), *riddings* (land which had been rid of trees) and burnt or brand lands. In Leighton the medieval waste was in the north of the parish, where field names like the 'Riddings', the 'Rough' and the 'Hurst' (a wooded knoll) abound, and where a deed of 1343 refers to 'an assart called Wygmorehurst towards Mount Gilbert' (the Wrekin). In Eaton Constantine the isolated farmstead called Ranslet is surrounded by fields incorporating the elements *wood, stocking* and *ridding* in their names, suggesting that it was established as part of the process of clearance. The many Shropshire farms called *Woodhouse* were probably established in the same way.

Some farms established during the process of clearance were moated. A survey has identified 115 moated sites in the county, 67 per cent of which are

18 *Fields around Ranslet Farm, Eaton Constantine.*

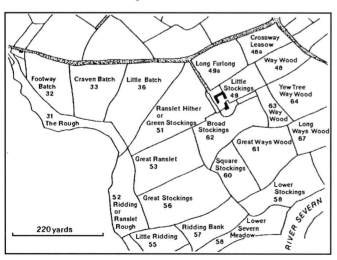

isolated from other settlements and seem to be associated with assarting. They are particularly prevalent in the areas of the North Shropshire plain which were brought into cultivation in the 13th and 14th centuries.

Large parts of Shropshire in the early middle ages were governed by forest laws designed to protect the king's hunting rights. Parts of Brewood Forest, particularly around Boscobel, and of the Wyre Forest on the Worcestershire border remain thickly wooded, but much of the Long Forest in the Hundred of Condover and of Mount Gilbert forest around the Wrekin were already under cultivation at the time of Domesday Book. Most such areas ceased to be forests in the legal sense in the 13th and 14th centuries.

19 *A cruck house in Much Wenlock.*

In several parts of Shropshire land which was too high or too wet for cultivation was used as common pasture. The parishes around Brown Clee shared grazing rights on the summit of the hill. The tenants who enjoyed such privileges were called *strakers* and a network of *outracks*, routes avoiding the normal road system of the district, enabled tenants from townships like Tugford, Holgate and Cold Weston not contiguous to the hill to take their beasts to the summit. The many small detached portions of parishes around the Brown Clee were probably watering places and overnight pastures for cattle bound to or from the summit. A similar system operated on the Weald Moors. A 17th-century document describes how the men of Wrockwardine were accustomed to take their beasts along Humbrey Lane, 'the direct Streake way from Wrockwardine Mannor House unto the Wildmoor', which ran past Allscott and through Long Lane to the Moor.

Much remains to be discovered about medieval housing in Shropshire. An excavation at Abdon in 1966-67 revealed the remains of a 13th-century long house which provided sparse accommodation. Few surviving houses can be dated earlier than the first part of the 14th century. Upper Millichope Farm is a stone hunting lodge of that period, as are the earliest of the many cruck-framed houses which have been identified in recent years. The larger houses of the late middle ages, like the 14th-century Manor House at Bedstone, contained some magnificent craftsmanship.

Many Shropshire townships which were communities of peasant farmers in the early middle ages are now isolated farmsteads, and some have disappeared altogether. Of the 70 hamlets in the hundred of Ford in 1086, nine are now totally deserted and 33 are single farms. All townships faced problems of survival during the period of falling population which extended from about 1350 to 1450. Some hamlets may have been depopulated by bubonic plagues in the mid-14th century. Some, like Berfield in Clun, may have been obliterated by Welsh raiders, and others, like Atcham and Shipton, were demolished to improve the environs of great houses. The majority declined slowly over several centuries. In the exposed parish of Cold Weston there were eight families in 1544, and four of the eight dwellings were demolished shortly before 1793. Nesse or Nash, one of the medieval hamlets of Wrockwardine, was the home of a farmer called Hercules Felton in 1668, but only a barn remained there by the mid-19th century.

20 *The roof of Manor Farm, Bedstone.*

The sites of some deserted villages, like Abdon, Cold Weston and Heath, are indicated by isolated churches, and many more are marked by house

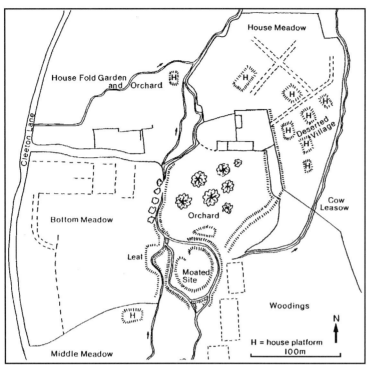

21 *The deserted settlement (SO607791) at Cleeton St Mary (after an original survey by Peter Hewitt).*

platforms, rectangular earthworks resulting from the gradual collapse of the houses. One of the best preserved deserted villages is Lawton, a township in Diddlebury parish by a bridge over the River Corve. A 'main street' of house platforms runs through an orchard to the village ponds, and a network of footpaths radiates from the bridge, from which can be seen what appear to be the remains of a mill mentioned in documents of the 14th century. Another impressive site is at Cleeton, well away from the Victorian village of Cleeton St Mary. At least eight platforms survive around hollow ways in a field called the House Meadow, between 200 and 300 yards from one of Shropshire's most spectacular moated sites.

Since the late middle ages the Shropshire landscape has been transformed by enclosure. While the open fields in the south Midland counties were largely enclosed by Act of Parliament in the 18th and 19th centuries, such legislation affected open fields in only seven Shropshire parishes. In most Shropshire parishes enclosure of the open fields seems to have taken place gradually and by consent some time between about 1450 and 1700, a change which was part of a substantial shift from arable to pastoral farming. In 1597 Sir Thomas Coningsby urged that Shropshire should be exempted from an enclosure bill encouraging the growth of corn because it was 'the dairy house of the whole realm'.

Many 16th- and 17th-century documents give impressions of open fields in which some groups of strips had been brought together by particular owners and fenced off, while other parts were still worked in the traditional manner. Open-field farming on the great estates of Whitchurch and Ellesmere was in an advanced state of decay by 1600. A glebe terrier for the parish of Leighton in 1612 refers to numerous hedges and enclosures within the three open fields. In the Field towards Buildwas, the vicar held 'One pyked Furlong lying with an enclosure near the meadow hedge'. Another terrier compiled in 1693 is written entirely in terms of an enclosed landscape. In Shifnal open-field farming was practised in the townships of Hatton, Stanton and Upton until the early 18th century but in hamlets like Woodhouses and Priorslee it had ceased much earlier. Many relics of open-field cultivation survived in Shropshire until the late 18th century or even into the 19th, but they were no more than relics. In most townships communal cultivation had ceased to be a reality by 1700.

I *Minsterley viewed from Pontesford Hill.*

II *Sheep grazing on the uplands of Clun Forest viewed from the ancient drovers' road which enters Shropshire at* The Anchor.

III *The Iron Bridge seen from the Rotunda (SJ669038), a belvedere on the limestone outcrop of Lincoln Hill which formed part of the network of Sabbath Walks laid out in the 1780s by the ironmaster, Richard Reynolds.*

IV *Ludlow from Whitecliff (S0505742) looking across the streets which slope down from the market area to the River Teme. In the centre is the chapel of St Thomas.*

6

The Church in the Middle Ages

The rôle of the church in medieval society was all-pervasive. The church was massively endowed. Its cathedrals and abbeys were the most imposing buildings of their time, and in the most remote parishes the church was the largest and most enduring building. Yet little is known of the details of church life in most communities, and the surviving medieval buildings remain the most eloquent memorials of an age of faith.

About one hundred Shropshire churches contain work from the 11th or 12th centuries. Some are substantial buildings like St Andrew, Shifnal, St George, Clun, St Peter, Wrockwardine and St Peter, Stanton Lacy, which were probably rebuildings of minster churches from which the surrounding country was served in Saxon times. Herring-bone masonry is a feature of the late 11th or early 12th centuries which can be found in the churches at Diddlebury, Clee St Margaret, Stanton upon Hine Heath, Rushbury, Sidbury and Culmington.

22 *The tiny medieval chapel at Langley in the parish of Acton Burnell (SJ537001).*

33

Further evidence of this period is to be found in the carved tympana in churches like Stottesdon and Aston Eyre, and in such remarkable fonts as those at Holy Trinity, Holgate and St Michael, Lilleshall. The tiny chapel at Heath is perhaps the most perfect Norman building of such a scale in England. The best 13th-century village church in Shropshire is St Mary, Acton Burnell, built by Robert Burnell, Chancellor of England and Bishop of Bath and Wells. The other outstanding rural church is St Bartholomew, Tong, built after 1410, to house a collegiate chantry. Shropshire was not a wealthy county in the later middle ages, and its village churches cannot compare with those of Lincolnshire, Norfolk or the Cotswolds.

Most of Shropshire's medieval town churches have disappeared. Of the four parish churches in Shrewsbury, only St Mary's, which is full of treasures of almost every phase of medieval architecture, still stands. Holy Trinity, Much Wenlock has much Norman and even some Saxon work. St Mary, Market Drayton, St Oswald, Oswestry, and St Nicholas, Newport have been heavily restored, and both of Bridgnorth's churches have been entirely rebuilt. St Laurence, Ludlow, ranks among the most beautiful parish churches in England. The church was already large by the end of the 12th century, but it is now largely the creation of the mid-15th century. Its crossing tower, its vaulting, its misericords, the scale of the nave, its memorials, its organ, are all of outstanding merit. Less spectacular, but of importance as a rare survival, is the chapel of St Thomas in Dinham, Ludlow, built about 1190. There were many such chapels in the larger medieval towns, among them those of St Nicholas, St Catherine, St Blaise, and St Mary Magdalen

23 The church of St Mary, Acton Burnell, built by Robert Burnell, Bishop of Bath and Wells and Chancellor of England, shortly after the middle of the 13th century (SJ533019).

24 *St Laurence, Ludlow, from the north east, drawn in 1812 (SO512746).*

25 *The soaring piers of the 15th-century nave and crossing of St Laurence, Ludlow (SJ512746).*

26 *The medieval church at St Martin's with its Perpendicular west tower, and its walls buttressed against the effects of mining subsidence (SJ323363).*

in Shrewsbury. St Chad's and St Mary's in Shrewsbury were collegiate churches, with many chantries erected to maintain prayers for the souls of deceased donors, and elaborate services sung by vicars choral.

There were 12 monasteries and a nunnery in Shropshire in the middle ages. The senior monasteries were those at Shrewsbury and Much Wenlock, both founded by Earl Roger of Montgomery between 1079 and 1083. Shrewsbury Abbey was a Benedictine house, which incorporated a small, pre-Conquest wooden church dedicated to St Peter. It was generously endowed, and gained prestige when the monks acquired the bones of St Winifred from Basingwerk in Flintshire about 1138. The Abbey had between 12 and 18 monks in the later middle ages. Its abbots were entitled to wear mitres from 1397, and regularly attended parliaments. At Much Wenlock Earl Roger re-founded the pre-Conquest abbey as a Cluniac priory. Wenlock promoted the cult of its seventh-century foundress, St Milburga, and its church was the largest monastic building in the county, some 106m long. The arcading and sculpture still to be seen are testimony to what must have been a breathtaking range of buildings, but features, like the clock tower for which Henry III gave six oak trees in 1233, are gone without trace. Wenlock probably had more monks than any other Shropshire house, with a total of about forty in the late 13th century. The one Cistercian abbey in the county was Buildwas. It was founded as a Savignac house by Roger de Clinton, Bishop of Chester, in 1135, but became a Cistercian abbey after the two orders were united in 1147. The other monasteries comprised the Benedictine priories of Morville and Bromfield, the Cluniac priory at Preen which was dependent on Wenlock, the Grandmontine house at Alberbury and the houses of Augustinian canons at Haughmond, Wombridge, Lilleshall, Ratlinghope and Chirbury. The solitary Shropshire nunnery was the Priory of St Leonard, Brewood, usually called 'White Ladies', a community of Augustinian canonesses established by 1186 in the extra-parochial liberty of Boscobel.

27 *Christ's entry into Jerusalem depicted on the Norman tympanum of the parish church at Aston Eyre.*

Monks were active in the colonisation of uncultivated land in many parts of Shropshire. Buildwas had granges at Hatton, Cosford and Ruckley on the edge of Brewood Forest, and was responsible for pushing back the frontiers of cultivation on the Stiperstones. Shrewsbury, Haughmond and Lilleshall had fulling mills, and the monasteries on the fringe of the Coalbrookdale coalfield were all operating bloomeries for making iron by the 1530s.

The first Dominican (or black) friars reached England in 1221, to be followed by the first group of Franciscan (or grey) friars in 1233. Within a few decades friaries were established in every town of consequence in England, usually just outside the walls. The first friars in Shropshire were the Dominicans, who built a friary in Shrewsbury on the slope between the walls and the Severn near St Mary's Water Lane in 1232. The Franciscans built friaries on the banks of the Severn at Bridgnorth in 1244 and west of the English Bridge in Shrewsbury by the following year. The Austin friars built a rural friary at Woodhouse near Cleobury Mortimer before 1250, and during the 1250s established themselves near the Welsh Bridge in Shrewsbury and outside the Galdeford Gate of Ludlow. A Carmelite friary was established by the Corve gate in Ludlow in 1350 with an exceptionally handsome range of buildings. Henry VI was entertained there, and John Leland called it a 'fair and costly thing'.

There were many other religious institutions in medieval Shropshire. The Knights Templar had a preceptory at Ludley near Cardington, founded in the 1160s. Roger de Powys, lord of Whittington, established a house of the Knights Hospitaller at Halston at much the same time. One of the most original religious foundations was the Palmers Guild of Ludlow, whose statutes date from 1284. The guild acquired extensive properties in Ludlow during the 14th century, and during the 15th its itinerant stewards recruited members in many parts of Britain. Some of the richest members provided money for masses or obits (annual memorial services) to be said on behalf of themselves and their kin. The guild helped to provide music in the church of St Laurence. In 1446-47 it purchased in Bristol 100 wainscot boards for the choir stalls which are still in the church. The guild provided a house for the grammar school in Ludlow by 1431, although it was not until some time between 1526 and 1533 that the school moved to its premises on the east side of Mill Street. Between 1462 and 1482 John Hosier, a member of the guild, endowed the almshouses which still bear his name. By the time of its dissolution in 1522 the guild possessed 152 tenements, 14 shops and 75 other premises in Ludlow, which passed to the borough corporation, which assumed the guild's responsibilities for the almshouses and the grammar school.

28 *Christ on the Lake—a carving of c.1180-1190 at Wenlock Priory.*

7

Towns of the Middle Ages

29 *The successful townsman, a misericord from the church of St Laurence, Ludlow*

Domesday Book records that there were only two boroughs in Shropshire in 1086, Shrewsbury and Quatford. The rest of the towns in the county, except for some of the commercial centres which grew up in the Coalbrookdale coalfield during the Industrial Revolution, were the result of deliberate plantation in the middle ages. Maurice Beresford's *New Towns of the Middle Ages* provides an illuminating language for the discussion of urban development which is particularly relevant in Shropshire.

Most of the new towns in Shropshire date from the period between the Norman Conquest and the mid-13th century. Some new towns were formally-planned additions to villages which already existed. Others are not mentioned in Domesday Book. They were new creations which were carved out of existing parishes. Many were built in the shadows of protecting castles. Ludlow was developed by the de Lacy family in the ancient parish of Stanton Lacy in the early 12th century. Bishop's Castle was laid out by the Bishop of Hereford in the parish of Lydbury North in the late 12th century. Bridgnorth was a plantation in Morville parish, which dates its origins from about 1101. Robert de Bellesme, son of Roger de Montgomery, probably transferred to the site the castle, church and borough recorded in Domesday Book at Quatford. Oswestry was founded by William FitzAlan in the late 12th century in the parish of Maesbury, adjacent to a castle which had been built before 1086. Newport was founded by King Henry I in the early 12th century, probably as a thoroughfare town where the north-south road could cross the wide marshes around the Strine Brook. The burgesses were committed to supply fish to the royal household, an obligation commemo-rated by the three fishes on the town's coat of arms, and by the dedication of the parish church to St Nicholas, patron saint of fishermen.

In those towns which were attached to existing villages contrasts can be observed between the formal layout of the new development and the haphazard pattern of building of the original settlement. At Clun, where a new town seems to have been built near the castle on the north bank of the river by the FitzAlans in the late 12th or early 13th century, the old village remains scattered around the church of St George on the south bank. Wellington was granted a charter for a market in 1244, probably soon after its foundation. The original plantation seems to have been a market place with a small grid of streets to the west, which remains distinct from what appears to be the original village settlement around the church. The expression 'new town' survived in field names in the Haygate Road area in the 19th century. At Madeley, which was probably founded by the monks of Wenlock some time before 1269, when the Prior was granted the right to hold markets and fairs, there remains a contrast between the formal layout of plots on High Street, and the random scatter of buildings around the parish church. Evidence of plantation is hard to find at Ellesmere, but medieval documents distinguish between an old town and a new town.

30 *An impression of the town at Richards Castle from a 17th-century map.*

Many planned boroughs failed to 'take-off' as towns. The monks of Lilleshall probably laid out a town by their toll bridge at Atcham where they were granted rights to hold fairs in 1269 and 1276. Shrewsbury Abbey established a new town at Baschurch where the right to hold fairs and markets was granted in 1256. Traces of deliberate planning can still be recognised in property boundaries in the area called New Town. The town failed, probably because a rival market grew up in the shadow of the castle at Ruyton, only two miles away. The Burnell family obtained a charter for a market and fair in their borough at Acton Burnell in 1269, but the town seems never to have flourished. Robert de Mortimer was granted a charter in 1216 for the town which had been laid out adjacent to the castle at Richards Castle. The borough and castle were in Herefordshire, but the bank which enclosed the town formed the boundary with Shropshire. The town flourished for a time but was falling into disuse by the early 14th century. The town established within the ramparts of the great castle at Caus was also initially successful. There were two gates, and a church dedicated to St Margaret which was distinct from the castle church of St Nicholas. The names of two thoroughfares, Castle Street and St Margaret Street, are known, and 54 tenements were occupied in the mid-14th century. The town declined in the late middle ages, and by 1541 there were only two tenants.

Ludlow is one of the best preserved medieval plantation towns in Europe and provides many examples of features which aid the understanding of other towns. The first component of the planned town was almost certainly the tract extending from the castle along the top of the promontory between the Teme and the Corve, which consisted of a wide market place, with long strips (called burgage plots) running north and south. The majority of Ludlow burgages have widths which are multiples of a perch (i.e. 16ft. 6ins., or 5m) and research elsewhere in the West Midlands confirms that this measurement was frequently used for such plots.

31 *The door by which the Augustinian canons of Lilleshall entered the Priory church from the cloisters. This pattern of doorway, with a segmental arch set within a semi-circular one, is widely used at Lilleshall.*

The sequence of later growth is not established, but it was clearly influenced by the pre-existing routeway following the line which is now Old Street and Corve Street. The lower part of Corve Street, more than a quarter of a mile from the castle, was laid out in burgage plots before 1186, and the enlargement of the parish church in 1199 strengthens the supposition that a sizeable town was then in existence. It was perhaps at about this time that Broad Street and Mill Street with their 'back lanes' were laid out. There may have been ambitious plans to create another grid of streets in the Linney parallel to Corve Street, but the western half of this area never attracted settlement. Nevertheless Ludlow was a successful plantation, and pressure on land in the town centre was intense, especially in the High

Street which had been colonised before 1270 by rows of stalls which later became permanent structures, with cellars below and solars above. As late as the 19th century one of these, adjacent to the Bull Ring, was known as 'the Shelds', a corruption of the Latin *selda*, stalls. Similar in-filled market places can be seen in Church Stretton and Wellington, while the pattern of a market place with a grid of streets to one side of it can be observed on a smaller scale at Bridgnorth and Clun. Many of Ludlow's burgage plots are filled with buildings at right angles to the frontage streets, a pattern which is repeated in every medieval town in Shropshire.

Some Shropshire towns were laid out along single main streets. The most perfectly preserved example is Bishop's Castle, where the back lanes at the ends of the burgage plots are all but complete. In most towns of this type there were 'island' buildings in the middle of the main streets. The parish church of St Nicholas, Newport and the town hall at Bishop's Castle are thus situated, and at Shifnal several such buildings grew up in the main street. They were a source of congestion by the early 19th century and the last were removed in the 1970s.

32 *Ludlow in the 1960s (SO514743) when the St John Street area outside the town walls was being rebuilt. In the top left-hand corner is the Castle. The original market place, now a maze of narrow lanes, extends along the plateau past the church of St Laurence to the ancient north-south main road. The grid of streets running from the market place to the Teme can clearly be distinguished, and the regular pattern of fields running north through the Linney towards the River Corve at the top of the picture suggests that there may have been plans to lay out streets in that area. Buildings on Old Street on the right of the picture include a cinema of the 1930s and a trouser factory of the 1950s and 1960s. In the very centre of the picture is Thomas Farnolls Pritchard's gazebo, illustrated on p.74.*

Most of Shropshire's larger medieval towns were surrounded by walls. The sections which survive mostly date from the 13th century as does the greater part of the documentary evidence relating to them. The walls of Ludlow date from 1233, long after the pattern of the town's streets had been established. Most of the circuit survives although parts are dilapidated. The north gate of Bridgnorth still stands after an early 20th-century rebuilding. It is possible to trace much of the course of the town's walls, but only fragments now remain. The complex walls of Shrewsbury are more difficult to trace, but one tower remains and several stretches have been temporarily uncovered during 20th-century building work. The walls of Oswestry have almost completely disappeared, but some

33 *The Toll Thorough which marks the site of the New Gate in the walls of Oswestry (SJ289295).*

sections have been identified during building operations. Wem was protected by three gates in the middle ages, possibly with an earthen bank linking them, and the survival of earthen enclosures at Caus and Richards Castle suggests that most planned boroughs may have had a measure of defensive protection. The example of Ludlow shows the many purposes to which town walls have been put since the middle ages. They have regularly been quarried for stone. Many buildings, particularly summer houses, are built on the tops of walls, and still more, including concrete garages and electricity sub-stations, lean against them.

The larger Shropshire towns all achieved a measure of self-government through charters of incorporation. Shrewsbury has a succession of charters, the first of them granted by Henry I. The town was empowered to choose bailiffs to head its government in the reign of King John, and it was one of the first boroughs to be represented in parliament in 1268 and 1283. Bridgnorth gained its first charter in 1157, two years after King Henry II took it during a siege. The borough returned members to parliament from 1295. Oswestry gained authority to administer its own affairs in 1399 after the Shrewsbury Parliament of the previous year had adjourned there. Ludlow Corporation was granted a charter by Edward IV in 1461, and the borough returned its first MPs in 1467.

Medieval houses survive in considerable numbers in Shrewsbury, Ludlow and Much Wenlock. In Wem, Newport, Oswestry, Bridgnorth and Shifnal many medieval buildings were destroyed by fires. The earliest houses

34 *The town of Much Wenlock (SJ625001) in the 1950s. In the foreground is the Prior's Lodge of c.1500, one of the finest English domestic buildings of the period. To the right are the ruins of the Cluniac priory church. At the centre is the parish church of Holy Trinity, and some of the streets of the little town at the priory gates. At the top are Victorian terraced cottages, and the railway yard in which a GWR tank locomotive, a set of passenger carriages and numerous freight wagons can be seen. The rural character of Much Wenlock is shown by the working farmyard above and to the right of the parish church.*

of which there is reliable evidence were the stone first-floor halls built by the more eminent citizens of Shrewsbury in the 13th century. The majority of medieval buildings are timber-framed, particular features being jetties, crown post roofs and spere trusses.

35 *The seal of the borough of Shrewsbury.*

Two Shropshire towns demand special attention. The *town* of Much Wenlock grew up at the gates of the priory. Its topography is difficult to explain, although elements of medieval planning can be observed there. It has always been a small town with a limited range of commercial facilities. The *borough* of Wenlock, by contrast, was in area the largest non-county borough in England. It was created by a charter of 1468 and comprised most of the extensive lands of the Cluniac priory of Wenlock, scattered as far afield as Little Wenlock in the north and Stoke St Milborough in the south. The borough courts had wide powers of jurisdiction, dealing with matters like coroners' inquisitions, which were usually the prerogative of Quarter Sessions. The charter granted the right to send one member to parliament, but two were being returned by the 1490s.

Shrewsbury is the other exception among Shropshire towns. It originated in the Saxon period, and its topography is for the most part inexplicable in terms of medieval plantation, although the borough of Abbey Foregate, a separate jurisdiction under the Abbot, was obviously a plantation, and the other extra-mural suburbs, Longden Coleham, Castle Foregate and Frankwell, appear to have been deliberately planned. Domesday Book reveals that the town had 252 houses, that the four parish churches were then in existence, and that the building of the Norman castle involved the destruction of 51 tenements. By the 13th century Shrewsbury was a large and prosperous town, with a population of between 3,000 and 4,000. Archaeological evidence suggests a substantial rebuilding in that period, with many alterations of levels, and resulting, most notably, in the creation of the space for fairs and markets now called The Square.

The poll tax returns of 1377 provide a measure by which to assess the national standing of Shropshire's medieval towns. It is estimated that Shrewsbury had a population of about 3,000, then ranking seventeenth amongst English provincial towns, just behind Gloucester and Leicester, but ahead of Exeter and Nottingham. Ludlow was ranked thirty-fourth, with an estimated population of 1,700, and Bridgnorth forty-first.

Much of the prosperity of these towns was based on wool, which was the chief cash product of rural Shropshire. Many of the early stages in the processing of wool and the making of cloth remained in the countryside, but the merchants who took most of the profits were townsmen. Surviving licences show that in 1273 English merchants exported nearly 5,000 sacks of wool, and that 660 of them were provided by Shropshire merchants, the largest total of any inland county. The most powerful of these merchants was Nicholas de Ludlow, whose base was at Shrewsbury although he maintained some commercial interests in the town from which he took his name. State papers record that in 1278 merchants from Flanders, the most important market for English wool, had to pay £2,022 to Nicholas de Ludlow, 'King's merchant'.

8

The Fluctuating Frontier

The Welsh Borderland in the middle ages was rarely untroubled by local disorders and was sometimes the scene of large-scale warfare with national implications. In some respects such disorders did no more than reflect the natural disaffinity between highlanders and lowlanders. To highlanders the rich arable and pastoral lands of the English Midlands presented a continuing temptation. Towns like Shrewsbury, Ludlow and Bridgnorth were rich beyond the imagination of those who lived in the hills. The borderland was also a nursery for the overmighty subject. Between territories which were obviously English or Welsh lay a buffer zone which came to be controlled by the Marcher lords, who were suffered by the English kings to exercise almost regal powers in return for preventing the incursions of the Welsh.

In 1086 Offa's Dyke formed the border between Shropshire and Wales, except for one small Welsh area east of the Dyke and the district around Montgomery which was then in Shropshire. In 1069 Edric the Wild, a Herefordshire thegn, attacked Shrewsbury. A period of guerrilla warfare followed, which William I brought to an end in 1070 by a campaign which devastated extensive stretches of countryside. By 1074 Roger de Montgomery, one of William I's closest Norman followers, had been created Earl of Shrewsbury, with powers which were intended to bring peace to the borderland.

During the 12th century the Marcher lordships emerged as buffers, almost indeed as independent states, between Welsh and English royal authority. The lordships resulted from the granting of privileges by the English Crown to the Marcher families, which led to the exclusion of the judicial authority of the monarch and of his representative the Sheriff of Shropshire from their domains. The Shropshire portion of the borderland was dominated by three great families. The FitzAlans, lords of Oswestry and Clun, came from the Cotentin peninsula in France and were probably in the service of Henry I before he became king. They acquired the lands which became the lordship of Oswestry in 1114. About 1155 the marriage of William FitzAlan to Isabel de Say brought them the lordship of Clun. It was probably during the second half of the 12th century that the FitzAlans withdrew Oswestry and the adjacent lordship of Ruyton-XI-Towns from the authority of the Sheriff of Shropshire, and by the mid-12th century they exercised similar powers in the lordship of Clun. The FitzAlans acquired great estates in southern England in 1243, but for a century afterwards they regarded themselves primarily as a Marcher family.

The Corbets of Caus dominated the central part of the Shropshire borderland from soon after the Conquest until the early 14th century. The castle of Caus, named after the Pays de Caux in Normandy, was probably built by Roger Fitz Corbet in the late 11th or early 12th century, superseding an earlier ring-work at Hawcocks Mount three quarters of a mile to the east, which stands in an enclosure which was called 'Alde-causefield' in 1361. By the 1230s, the Corbets succeeded in withdrawing from royal jurisdiction large parts of the hundreds of Chirbury and Ford. After the death of Peter Corbet in 1322 the Mortimers and FitzAlans strove to gain control of his lands but were thwarted by his widow.

The Mortimers of Wigmore settled in the borderland a generation earlier than the FitzAlans but it was chiefly due to Roger Mortimer, Lord of Wigmore from 1246-1282, that they became one of the most powerful families in the Marches. He took advantage of the turmoil caused by the rising of Simon de Montford in the 1260s to gain the manors of Cleobury Mortimer and Chelmarsh. His powers were checked in the reign of Edward I. Roger Mortimer, first Earl of March, was born in 1286 or 1287. By 1306 he had gained possession of Ludlow Castle by his marriage. With his mistress, the Queen, he plotted the overthrow of Edward II. In the later 14th and 15th centuries the Mortimers were one of the most powerful families in the kingdom.

36 The round Norman chapel in Ludlow Castle (SO508746) which dates from the mid-12th century.

The lands of most English barons were dispersed, but the Marcher lordships were concentrated. It was essential in the borderland to maintain fighting troops, who could, when occasion arose, be used in conflicts with political opponents in England. Both the FitzAlans and the Mortimers held the office of Sheriff of Shropshire and used it to increase their own powers. All the principal Marcher lords held lands which were Welsh, where they collected the traditional dues paid to Welsh lords, and others which were English where they received the feudal incomes collected by lords in other parts of the kingdom. They gained profits from their courts, from sheep farming and the founding of towns. The lordships caused confusion in the administration of the criminal law. A man accused of a crime could flee from one lordship to another, or gain entry into one of them from Shropshire, and would often receive sanctuary.

37 Arcading in the ruined chapter house of the Cluniac Priory of Much Wenlock.

In the 13th century many of the principal dramas of national politics were enacted in the borderland or with borderland players in leading rôles. King John, having assembled an army at Oswestry, personally led two incursions into Wales in 1211 and took 20 hostages. The following year the Welsh under Llewellyn ab Iorwerth stormed John's newly-built castle at Aberystwyth, in response to which the king put to death the hostages, one of them, Rhys ap Maelgw aged seven, being publicly executed in Shrewsbury. Three years later as the ally of the barons who gained Magna Carta from John, Llewellyn occupied Powys and took possession of Shrewsbury.

King Henry III was frequently in Shropshire while engaged in military operations against, or negotiations with, the Welsh. During the king's minority in 1221 a treaty was signed in Shrewsbury between the English and Llewellyn ab Iorwerth. Two years later Llewellyn captured the castles of Kinnerley and Whittington. In 1230-31 Llewellyn and his allies laid waste parts of the Marches, and in 1233 burnt Oswestry and Clun and occupied Shrewsbury. A peace settlement was reached at Myddle in June 1234. Llewellyn ab Iorwerth, known as Llewellyn the Great, died in 1240, and the following year Henry III marched with an army from Gloucester to Shrewsbury to quell the threat of armed incursions from his son David. During the wars in the 1260s between the king and the baronial opposition led by Simon de Montfort, Shrewsbury, Ludlow and Richards Castle were seized by Simon's followers, and there was a contingent of Welsh in the baronial army which was defeated in the Battle of Evesham in 1265. Llewellyn ap Gruffydd, grandson of Llewellyn ab Iorwerth, received the homage of most of the lesser Welsh princes in 1258, and began to threaten English authority in the borderland. In 1267 Henry III and the papal legate Cardinal Ottobon were in Shrewsbury, but military action was deferred and the Treaty of Montgomery brought peace to the region for a time.

Two years later the Lord Edward, son of Henry III, was given charge of Shrewsbury, and after his accession to the throne as Edward I in 1272 his campaigns frequently brought him to Shropshire. The king announced his intention of making war on Llewellyn ap Gruffydd at Michaelmas 1276. His army assembled at Worcester in July 1277 and passed through Shropshire, making their main bases at Oswestry and Montgomery. For some months in 1277 the courts of the Exchequer and King's Bench sat in Shrewsbury. Llewellyn submitted in November as Edward's army besieged Snowdonia, and the English king began the construction of new castles at Rhuddlan, Flint, Aberystwyth and Builth. Fighting resumed in the spring of 1282 when an English army under the Earl of Gloucester was defeated at Llandeilo and Oswestry was sacked immediately before Easter. In December Llewellyn was killed by a Shropshire soldier, Stephen Frankton, near Builth. King Edward embarked on another siege of Snowdonia with the object of starving into submission the Welsh army, now led by Llewellyn's brother David, who was captured, following the collapse of organised resistance, in June 1283. The following autumn a parliament was summoned at Shrewsbury and adjourned to Acton Burnell, the manor of Robert Burnell, Chancellor of England, where the lords sat in the hall of the castle and the commons in a nearby barn. The main business of the parliament was the trial of David ap Gruffydd, who, as a baron of the English realm, was accused of treason. He was sentenced to be dragged at a horse's tail through the streets of Shrewsbury, to be hanged, to have his heart and intestines burnt, to have his head cut off and his body quartered. The four quarters were exhibited in different parts of the kingdom, and the heads of David and his brother Llewellyn were displayed at the ends of lances at the Tower of London.

38 *The gable end wall of the barn near Acton Burnell Castle (SJ533018) where it is supposed that the House of Commons assembled in the parliament of 1283.*

The numerous castles in Shropshire are evidence of the warfare which raged along the border in the middle ages. There are several Saxon fortified sites in the county, and just beyond the border Richards Castle was built about 1050 by Richard son of Scrob, one of the Normans who came to England in the reign of Edward the Confessor. Like many later castles, this consisted of a mount or motte, adjacent to which was a courtyard enclosed by a ditch and rampart known as a bailey. More than 150 such castles were built in Shropshire in the century or so after the Norman Conquest. One group, situated between Montgomery and Caus, have uniform features, with mottes three to six metres high with diameters at the tops of six to seven metres. It has been suggested that they were built in the late 11th century when the region was resettled after the devastation recorded in Domesday Book.

Motte and bailey castles were probably not permanently occupied, but Mr. P.A. Barker's long-sustained excavations at Hen Domen have shown that their building histories were complicated. New castle building from the mid-12th century was largely in stone. Most castles of the reign of Henry II had massive keeps which served as the last strongholds of the fortifications, and also contained residential accommodation. Most such keeps, those at Ludlow, Bridgnorth, Hopton Castle and Clun

39 *The great hall, west wall and towers of Acton Burnell Castle (SJ532018).*

for example, are rectangular in plan, although that at Richards Castle, built about 1175, was octagonal. New construction of the early 13th century consisted largely of round or semi-circular towers like those which survive at Shrewsbury, Whittington and Clun.

The conclusion of Edward I's conquest of Wales is reflected in a change in the character of castle building. In 1280 Robert Burnell rebuilt the castle at Holgate. As Chancellor of England he was aware of the castles being built in North Wales by Edward I and, hidden by a 17th-century farm-house, there still stands one tower of his castle, with masonry of superlative quality, comparable with that at Caernarvon or Conway. Just a few years later, in 1284, after the conclusion of the wars, Burnell began the castle at Acton Burnell. It is a large rectangular house, with round towers projecting at each corner. It is moatless and the doorways are on the ground floor, not at first-floor level like that at Shrewsbury Castle. Almost contemporary with Acton Burnell is Stokesay Castle which is likewise a fortified dwelling house. Its hall, whose great windows render it scarcely defensible, was probably built in the 1270s. Its builder, the wool merchant Laurence de Ludlow, received a licence to crenellate the house in 1291 when he probably added another tower. In the 14th century additions continued to be made to the large stone castles like Shrewsbury and Ludlow for residential purposes.

The borderland in the 14th and 15th centuries was dominated by the great Marcher families and particularly by the Mortimers and the FitzAlans. In 1398 parliament was adjourned from London to Shrewsbury Abbey, where Lords and Commons met amid sumptuous splendour. The following year Richard II was replaced by the usurper Henry Bolingbroke, who became Henry IV. Early in his reign there was a rising of the Welsh led by Owen Glendower, owner of lands in the Dee valley. After an inconclusive campaign

40 The church of St Mary Magdalene, Battlefield (SJ513173), which was erected by Roger Ive in 1406 to enable masses to be said for the souls of those slain in the Battle of Shrewsbury on 22 July 1403. It was restored in 1861 by the Shrewsbury architect, Samuel Pountney Smith, who installed a magnificent pavement of Jackfield tiles in the chancel.

in 1402, Glendower gained as an ally Henry Percy, Earl of Northumberland, who had been one of Henry IV's principal accomplices in the usurpation of Richard II. Percy's son, Hotspur, led an army southward, and was defeated and killed at the Battle of Shrewsbury on 11 July 1403. After the battle Glendower retreated into Wales, where, in spite of further English campaigns, he retained his estates until his death in 1414. On the site of the encounter with Hotspur, Roger Ive, a member of a prominent Shrewsbury family, built a chapel dedicated to St Mary Magdalene in 1406 to enable masses to be said for the souls of the slain, and received a royal endowment for it in 1410. The tower was not completed until the early 16th century. The roof of the church collapsed and it was little more than a ruin by 1800, but it was restored in 1861-62 by the architect Samuel Pountney Smith.

There were many conflicts in the Marches during the Wars of the Roses in the mid-15th century. In the 1450s Ludlow was the base of Richard, Duke of York, who challenged the rule of Henry VI. In 1459 Ludlow was the projected rendezvous for the troops of the Earl of Warwick, who had come to England from Calais, with those of the Duke of York. In the event there were battles with the Lancastrians at Blore Heath near Market Drayton, which the Yorkists won in September, and at Ludford, which the Yorkists lost in October, after which Ludlow was pillaged. The following year the Duke of York was killed in the Battle of Wakefield, but his son Edward, Earl of March, beat the Lancastrians at Mortimers Cross near Ludlow in February 1461 and soon afterwards was proclaimed King Edward IV. Shrewsbury was of particular importance in the campaign of Henry, Earl of Richmond, to wrest the crown from Richard III in 1485. After landing from France at Milford Haven, Richmond found that Shrewsbury was the only crossing point on the Severn not held by his enemies. He was received in the town with enthusiasm and advanced to defeat Richard and to gain the crown as Henry VII at Bosworth Field.

41 *The gatehouse at the Council Headquarters of the Council in the Marches and Wales in Shrewsbury.*

During the 16th century the turbulence of the Marches was gradually suppressed. The endemic casual violence, the murders and cattle rustling were quelled by the Council in the Marches and Wales. In 1471 Edward IV had established a council to look after the affairs of the infant Prince of Wales. In 1476 it was given a judicial commission covering Shropshire, Herefordshire, Gloucestershire and Worcestershire. Henry VII gave similar powers to the council of Arthur, Prince of Wales, in 1493, and by 1501 a council for the Prince was formally appointed, and Arthur was sent to rule Wales from Ludlow. In the next reign in 1525 Cardinal Wolsey dispatched Princess Mary to Ludlow with a council which was both a household, responsible for the princess's education, and a court with authority to administer justice. In 1534 Thomas Cromwell appointed Rowland Lee, Bishop of Coventry and Lichfield, as President of the Council. He saw the main problem in the Marches as the suppression of murder and theft and used public hangings as a deterrent to both crimes. It was remarked when he died in 1543 that he 'brought Wales, beinge at hys fyrst comy'ge very wylde, in good syvilitie before he dyed, who said he would macke the whyte sheepe keep the blacke'.

HEERE LYE ŦE BODIES OF EDMVND
WALTR ESŒVIER CHIEFFE IVSTICE OF
ŦREE SHIERS IN SOVŦ WALES AND
ONE OF HIS MA^{TES} COVNCILL IN ŦE
MARCHES OF WALES AND OF MARY
HIS WIFE DAVGHTER OF THOMAS
HACKLVIT OF EYTON ESŒVIER
WHO HAD ISSVE ŦREE SONNES NAMED
IAMES IOHN AND EDWARD AND
TWO DAVGHTERS NAMED MARY
AND DOROŦY HE WAS BVRIED ŦE
XXIX. DAYE OF IANVARIE-ANN:DNI:1592

The Council performed important functions in criminal, civil and ecclesiastical law. Neither its powers nor the area over which it had authority were precisely defined. Ludlow was the base of the Council's operations, and the memorials of its chief officers and their families adorn the church of St Laurence. The Council had quarters in Shrewsbury in the range of buildings which is still called the Council House. In April 1581 Sir Henry Sidney, president of the Council, was in Shrewsbury, where he was regaled with processions, pageants and banquets, and left in a barge to the sound of cannon firing and of madrigals sung by scholars of Shrewsbury School, arrayed in green with green willows on their heads. The Council was suspended during the Interregnum, and after a revival under Charles II was finally dissolved in 1689.

If the Council was responsible for the suppression of endemic crime in the Marches, the statute of 1536 incorporating Wales and England brought an end to the propensity of the region to act as a nursery for overmighty subjects. Through other legislation during the next ten years, the lands which had comprised the lordships of Oswestry, Knockin, Maesbrook Whittington, Clun and Ellesmere were brought under the jurisdiction of the county authorities, and the Welsh shires of Radnor, Montgomery and Denbigh were defined.

42 *The alabaster tomb of Edmund Walter, Chief Justice of South Wales and a member of the Council in the Marches and Wales, in the chancel of the church of St Laurence, Ludlow. In spite of the inscription, Walter died in 1594. The tomb was provided for in the will of Edmund's son, James Walter, who died in 1625.*

43 *A chapel in Oswestry used by a Welsh-speaking Non-conformist congregation.*

The new border reflected the extent of the lordships rather than linguistic or racial realities. The vicar of Whittington kept a Welsh-speaking curate until the late 18th century. Welsh services were maintained at Oswestry parish church until 1814, and in 1821 the chapel at Trefonen was built to accommodate Welsh-speakers in the parish. In 1872 Welsh services commenced in the Victoria Rooms in the centre of Oswestry, which led to the building of the church of St David in 1912. In the 1880s Welsh services were still being performed at Llanyblodwell and in Non-conformist chapels around Oswestry, but it was thought that Welsh was no longer used in churches or in the private homes of native inhabitants anywhere east of Oswestry.

The border wars left an impression on Shropshire's ecclesiastical geography. In the 11th century the county lay within the dioceses of Hereford and Lichfield, but in the second half of the 12th century during a period of Welsh predominance the parishes around Oswestry became part of the diocese of St Asaph, in which they remained until the disestablishment of the Church of Wales in 1920, when they reverted to the care of the Bishop of Lichfield.

By 1550 the state of the castles in the borderland reflected the region's transformation. Ludlow, seat of the Council in the Marches, remained a magnificent spectacle, the scene of pageantry and luxury. At Corfham only one precarious tower remained of the great stone castle. The lead had been removed from the roof, and the courtyards were 'all decayed, ruinated and destroyed'. John Leland found at Richards Castle 'The kepe, the waulls and towres of yt yet stond, but goynge to ruyn. There is a poore house of timber in the castle garth for a farmer'. At Oswestry a surveyor in 1602 noted 'great waste done upon the castle as well in stone and lead as in iron and timber', and he reflected that the castle had been garrisoned 'in times of the Welsh tumults which in times past were verie common'. The disorder which had been characteristic of Shropshire's western borderland for centuries had effectively been subdued.

9

Revival and Reformation

The changes which occurred in Shropshire between 1530 and the outbreak of the Civil War were as momentous as those in any county in England. The so-called Acts of Union of 1536 and 1542 brought an end to the Marcher lordships. The activities of the Council in the Marches brought a measure of order to the region which it had lacked throughout the middle ages. The towns gained new levels of prosperity expressed in many fine buildings. The dissolution of the monasteries brought many of their estates into the hands of ambitious men anxious to improve them.

44 *Plaish Hall (SO529965), built for Sir William Leighton in the 1540s, the first notable brick house in the county.*

Research has suggested that the second half of the 15th century was a period of economic decline in Shrewsbury when trade may have fallen by as much as 70 per cent. A statute of the early 16th century numbered Shrewsbury, Bridgnorth and Ludlow amongst towns where many tenements were 'in great ruin and decay'. Some of this decline may have been due to the loss of Shrewsbury's traditional victualling trade with Wales, which was said at different times to have been taken by Oswestry, Welshpool, Bishop's Castle and Whitchurch, but it is more likely that it reflected demographic factors which probably affected every town in the county. The lapse of the market at Ellesmere was blamed on plague. After 1550 there are signs of recovery.

In the late 1530s the monasteries were suppressed. Thomas Cromwell's commissioners sent to examine them found some once flourishing religious houses were in decline. Water was pouring into the choir of the Abbey church in Shrewsbury through a hole in the roof. One of the few scandals was at the Austin friary in Shrewsbury, where the prior, 'a man like to be in a frenzy', was selling the goods of the house, there was neither food,

45 *Stokesay Castle (SO435816), showing the tower and the great hall, and the medieval church of St John the Baptist.*

drink nor bedding, and only two friars were in residence, both of them Irish. After the dissolution most monastic buildings fell into ruin, but part of the Abbey in Shrewsbury, and the churches at Bromfield, Chirbury, Morville and Battlefield became parish churches. Consideration was given for a time to the alteration of diocesan boundaries, and the Abbey church in Shrewsbury and the priory church at Much Wenlock were regarded as potential cathedrals.

The parish clergy of Shropshire seem to have accepted the kaleidoscopic changes in officially sanctioned religious observances of the mid-16th century with little protest. In 1536 the authority of the Pope was formally abolished, and the clergy were instructed to teach in English, using the Coverdale Bible which had appeared in 1535, and to remove images from their churches. With the accession of Queen Mary I in 1553, the Latin Mass was restored. The accounts of St Mary's, Shrewsbury record the re-erection of altars and the rood, and the purchase of tapers, candles and frankincense following Mary's accession. When she was succeeded by her Protestant sister Elizabeth in 1558 the rood and the altars were soon removed. Some Shropshire gentry, like Sir Andrew Corbet of Moreton Corbet, encouraged Puritan ministers in their parishes, and Puritan clergy in Shrewsbury drew large congregations. John Tomkiss, incumbent of St Mary's who lived in the Drapers' Hall, was renowned as a 'painful' preacher. The destruction of the relics of medieval superstition continued. In 1584 some stained glass windows and a stone altar were removed from St Mary's, and during the 1580s the crosses outside St Mary's and St Julian's were destroyed.

46 *An allegorical figure which forms part of the stonework of the Elizabethan range of Moreton Corbet Castle (SJ561231), built by Sir Andrew Corbet from 1579.*

The consequences of the dispersal of land in Shropshire which had previously been held by the monasteries were profound. Either directly after the dissolution or gradually during the subsequent decades, large areas came into new hands, often those of London lawyers. As early as 1539 the estates of Lilleshall Abbey passed to James Leveson, whose family, with others, were active in subsequent decades in attempts to drain the Weald Moors, digging dykes and building bridges, blocking and destroying those made by others, and attempting to exclude tenants in adjacent parishes who claimed rights of common. Leveson's descendants were successively created Barons Gower in 1703, Earls Gower in 1746, Marquesses of Stafford in 1786 and Dukes of Sutherland in 1833.

47 *The early 17th-century manor house at Cherrington.*

Thomas Egerton, a member of a family of Cheshire gentry who became Attorney-General, Master of the Rolls and Lord Keeper, bought the Whitchurch estate, consisting of about 30,000 acres (12,000 ha.) in 1598, and the Ellesmere estate of about 8,900 acres (3,600 ha.) in 1600. They proved profitable investments. Rents were increased, and tenants were forced to apply lime and compost to their land. Egerton died in 1617 and his son became Earl of Bridgewater after inheriting his estates.

John Weld, like Egerton, came from a family of Cheshire gentry. His two sisters married Humphrey Slaney and William Whitmore, both members of prominent Shropshire landed families. Weld was a lawyer, who by purchase became Town Clerk of London in 1613. He bought the Willey estate in Shropshire in 1618, the manor of Marsh in 1619, and a third part of the manor of Broseley in 1620, becoming within a short time one of the principal landowners in the Shropshire coalfield. About 1631 he fell ill and wrote a memorandum, recommending to his descendants ways of increasing the income from the estate. He contemplated building a glass house at Willey and foresaw a time when iron might be smelted with coal.

48 *Late afternoon winter sunshine makes visible the remnants of ridge-and-furrow cultivation near Benthall Hall (SJ658026).*

The 16th century was a time of agricultural change in Shropshire, as the county came to concentrate increasingly on pastoral farming. Much enclosure took place in the lordship of Oswestry. In the parish of Myddle about 1,000 acres of mere, marsh and sandy waste were brought into cultivation between the late 15th century and the mid-17th. In Myddle Wood 241 acres were cleared by renting plots to freeholders and tenants in the adjacent townships in lieu of common rights. The glacial lakes known as Myddle Pool were drained about the 1570s, and Harmer Moss was cleared of its water and turf and made into meadow and pasture in the years after 1617.

Other areas of waste were settled by squatters, landless men who built houses on common land and enclosed small plots around them. The earliest documentary record of squatting in Shropshire is in Kenley, where there was an isolated cottage on the common by 1537 which had been joined by 12 others by 1600. In 1747 there were 31 cottages in the area, with holdings of up to 12 acres. Common land, whether open heathland, wayside verges or village greens, was owned by the lords of manors, although they could not sell or rent it. They could impose annual fines upon squatters who encroached upon it, and in the course of time the names of squatters were often entered upon rent rolls. It was often therefore in the interest of the lord to allow squatting. Squatters settled around the edges of large commons like those on Hayton's Bent, Catherton, or Pontesbury Hill, moving slowly away from the edges, creating mazes of rough tracks between the boundaries of their tiny fields. Occasionally a bold spirit would plant his cottage on an 'island' away from his neighbours in the middle of a common.

49 *A squatter cottage of early 19th-century date from Little Dawley, in the Blists Hill open air museum.*

Squatters also built cottages on village greens, as at Tugford, where they were forcibly removed in the early 17th century, and in 'slangs', long narrow strips of land alongside roads. Many cottages in slangs can still be seen in the north of the county. Squatter hedges usually grow from the low earthen banks which were the first hastily dug boundaries of each enclosure, and were made up of plants which were useful or saleable, like hazel, damson, sloe, crab apple, rowan and holly. Squatter cottages were usually crudely built, and often have a large chimney stack at one end. If they were of stone the walls were thick and far from square. Roof timbers were often unsawn, and most floors were probably originally of earth. Many squatter cottages were built of turf and have long since disappeared. One at Adston built in a slang by the Moorhouse Brook on the border of Wentnor by John Overton about 1746 was no longer occupied by 1812 but a turf cottage at Loughton was still inhabited in 1861.

Squatting occurred in all parts of the county. In the lordship of Oswestry six cottagers who had settled in the Forest of Treflach were said to be 'noisome neighbours unto the forests for their goats confound the underwoods as fast as they grow'. There were few attempts to prevent squatting in the parish of Myddle, where cottagers who were weavers, tailors, bakers and carpenters provided many skills upon which tenants and freeholders were able to call. Richard Gough describes how Evan Jones, a Welshman, 'built a lytle hutt upon Myddle Wood neare the Clay lake, att the higher end of the towne, and incloased a peice out of the common'. The wife of another squatter, who kept an alehouse, supplemented the family income by baking cakes which won a high reputation.

50 *An improvised join in the roof of the squatter cottage from Little Dawley in the Blists Hill open air museum.*

Some of the educational and charitable functions which had been performed by the religious houses were continued by other means after the Reformation. In Bridgnorth there was a grammar school by about 1503, which was endowed by the middle of the century. In Oswestry, a school which existed in the early 15th century was being supported in 1548 by money which had previously maintained a chantry in the parish church. In

Ludlow the corporation supported the grammar school after it received the properties of the Palmers Guild in 1552. In Newport a school which had been taught by a chantry priest survived the Reformation, and with a small endowment continued until 1878. After the establishment of a grammar school by William Adams, a London Haberdasher in 1656, the older foundation was known as the English School. In Whitchurch and Market Drayton schools were established by Sir John Talbot and Sir Rowland Hill in the mid-16th century. By the end of the 16th century there were schools in most Shropshire towns, and also in a few villages like Bitterly, Worfield, and Donnington in the parish of Wroxeter. At the latter, established in 1627, the first master, John Owen, had amongst his pupils the future Lord Newport, the Puritan divine Richard Baxter, and Richard Allestree, later Provost of Eton.

The school established in 1552 by the petition of the citizens of Shrewsbury was the most important of these post-Reformation foundations. It was first endowed with £20 a year from the estates of the colleges of St Mary and St Chad, which was augmented in 1571 by the rectory of Chirbury and other tithe incomes which had belonged to the priory of Chirbury. In 1561, Thomas Ashton, a graduate of the Puritan-inclined St John's College, Cambridge, was appointed headmaster, and under his guidance the school grew rapidly in size and reputation. In 1581 there were 360 pupils and five years later it was said to be the largest school in England. Ashton ceased to be headmaster in 1571, but he seems to have been responsible for the instruments under which the school was governed which were drawn up in 1572 and 1578. They provided for a close association with St John's College, which was able to appoint masters and offered closed scholarships. In 1595 new buildings on the scale of a contemporary Oxford or Cambridge college were commenced. The school flourished during most of the 17th century but from the 1680s it entered a period of decline, and for much of the 18th century it enjoyed no higher a reputation than the grammar schools in the smaller Shropshire towns. In Ashton's time, however, its pupils included Sir Philip Sidney and Sir Fulke Greville, and Ashton's Whitsuntide plays, in which he took 'marvellous greate paynes', won it great celebrity.

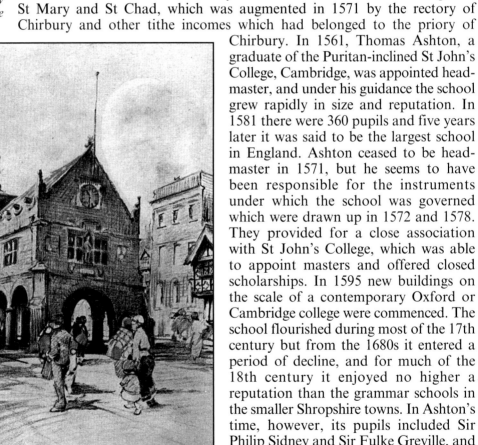

51 *Shrewsbury's Elizabethan market hall in the Square (SJ494127), built by the stone mason Walter Hancock in 1596-97 (from a sketch in Shropshire County Library by Marjorie C. Bates).*

52 *The guild hall of the Shrewsbury Drapers' Company. The main building was erected in the 1570s, and the narrow, taller block over the porch in the following decade (SJ494125).*

Much of the distinctive character of Ludlow in the 16th and early 17th centuries was derived from the Council in the Marches which had its head-quarters at the castle. Some of the judges and many attorneys, pursuivants and clerks lived in the town, and provided a market for local service trades which helped to cushion the economy against the decline of the cloth industry after 1600. In the 16th century cloth production in Ludlow ranged between 400 and 800 pieces a year, many of them being coarse cloths called 'Ludlow Whytes' which in the 1590s were selling in London for £2 10s. 0d. each. By 1610 output had slumped to less than 100 cloths. Ludlow's prosperity was marked by many splendid timber buildings ornamented by herring-bone struts, intricately carved star panels and beam ends, and elaborate barge boards. The most memorable of these buildings is now the *Feathers Hotel*.

In Shrewsbury the same period saw much building activity. The area around The Square retains many fine domestic buildings like Owen's and Ireland's mansions, although some of the best Elizabethan houses in the town have long since been demolished. Between 1552 and 1579 a supply of water from a spring two miles to the south west was brought to conduits in the town centre, and in 1596-98 the market hall in The Square was constructed, probably by the mason Walter Hancock.

Shrewsbury's prosperity in the late 16th and 17th centuries was based on trade in Welsh cloth handled by the Drapers' Company which had been founded by Edward IV, and came to dominate the town's affairs in the reign of Elizabeth. In the 1580s the Drapers were buying cloth in Oswestry, taking it to Shrewsbury, having it finished by shearmen in the town, and then transporting it to London for export to the poorer countries of Europe. An order of 1583 prohibited any Draper from crossing the Welsh Bridge en route to Oswestry until the bell tolled at six o'clock. The Drapers successfully excluded the Shrewsbury Mercers' Company from any share in their trade and, after a series of legal and parliamentary struggles, gained a virtual monopoly in the trade in 1621, which was the more effective because it was entirely *de facto*, and did not depend on a statute which could be repealed. It became customary for Welsh clothiers to bring their cloth to Shrewsbury for a market which was held in The Square on Thursdays. In 1576 the Drapers built a new guild hall in St Mary's Place, and many of the best houses in the town of the period were built for members of the company.

Many of Shropshire's most distinguished country houses were built in the late 16th and the early 17th centuries. Some of the mansions of the period were timber-framed. Pitchford Hall was built by John Sandford, 'carpenter of Salop', for Adam Ottley, a Shrewsbury merchant, in the 1560s and '70s, to an E-plan, with jetties, many herring-bone struts, and spectacular star-shaped chimney stacks. Park Hall, Whittington dated from the same period and was even larger, but was destroyed by fire in 1919. The range added by Sir Andrew Corbet to Moreton Corbet Castle in the 1570s was one of the most magnificent buildings of its period in England. The first notable Shropshire house in which brick was employed was Plaish Hall, built by Sir William Leighton in the 1540s. The mason Walter Hancock built the mansion at High Ercall for the Newport family, and probably constructed Condover Hall for Thomas Owen in the 1590s. Of the vast mansion which the Newports built at Eyton on Severn only one small tower and some fragments incorporated into a farmhouse now remain. It was probably the grandest house of its period in the county.

53 *Pitchford Hall (SJ548042), the most spectacular Tudor house in Shropshire, built for Adam Ottley, probably in the 1560s.*

10

The Civil War

None of the decisive set-piece battles of the English Civil War took place in Shropshire, yet the control of the county's towns and castles, its industrial resources and the routes which passed through it was significant in the war, and the conflict made a deep impression on Salopians. Richard Gough in his *History of Myddle* frequently makes the war a point of reference, and shows an acute perception of the issues at stake.

The predominant opinion among the county community in Shropshire was for the king rather than for parliament, although this feeling was not unanimous. Of the 12 Shropshire members of the Long Parliament, eight fought on the king's side and four for parliament. In Shrewsbury especially, King Charles's exactions of Ship Money in the 1630s had aroused considerable opposition, and Puritan sympathies were strong amongst the town's ruling élite.

The most dramatic event of the war in Shropshire was the appearance of King Charles in the county immediately before the outbreak of hostilities. The king had raised his standard at Nottingham on 13 September 1642, and then proceeded through Derby to Wellington on 19 September, where he was met by Sir John Weld. The following morning he reviewed his troops below the Wrekin and went on to Shrewsbury. Before his arrival there had been doubt about the fate of the magazine which was kept in the county town and about the allegiance of the population. It now appears that Sir Richard Newport persuaded the king to go to Shropshire on the promise of delivering over the county to him, for which he sought and received a peerage.

While the king was in Shrewsbury the court was established at the Council House. Courtiers were lodged with leading citizens, and the surrounding fields were used for the drilling of soldiers under the command of Prince Maurice and Prince Rupert. On 21 September it was estimated that the king had a force of 6,000 men. Gentry made their way to the town with gifts of plate and money. The universities sent plate and that belonging to Shrewsbury School was handed over by the headmaster. The mint, for which this silver was accumulated, was set up under the superintendence of Thomas Bushell, but it did not start work until after the king's departure. While he was in Shrewsbury King Charles renewed the town's charter, and issued his Solemn Protestation, blaming any future hostilities on others. On 12 October he left, proceeding through Bridgnorth and Wolverhampton on

54 *Star panels and a window sill dropped below the level of the horizontal frame member, in Bishop Percy's house, Bridgnorth, of 1580.*

a journey which took him to the battlefield of Edgehill on 23 October. After an inconclusive conflict Charles advanced towards London but was checked at Turnham Green. He retired to make his headquarters at Oxford.

Shrewsbury was garrisoned as one of the king's strongpoints. The castle was strengthened, and houses in its vicinity demolished. The walls were renewed, and an artillery base established at Cadogan's Fort above Frankwell. In 1643 Sir Fulke Hunkes was appointed governor, but he was regarded by some Royalist gentry as too sympathetic to the Puritans, and was replaced by Sir Francis Ottley, who in turn was succeeded by Sir Michael Earnley. Thomas Bushell dispatched the money-striking equipment from the mint on 20 December and those conveying it were entertained with sack and burnt claret by the corporation of Bridgnorth. On 3 January 1642-43, with more than a dozen carts, they straggled into Oxford.

The English Civil War was not a conflict with rigid fronts, mass armies and solidly occupied territories. It was a war within a community, in which there was substantial support for both sides in most parts of the kingdom. It was closer in character to the hostilities in Vietnam in the 1960s and '70s than to the world wars of the 20th century. It was a war of sieges, concerned with the holding of key towns and strategic routes. North Wales was the one substantial part of the kingdom where there was no significant support for parliament, and the control of Shropshire was therefore vital to the king to maintain his links with an important recruiting area, as well as to keep in contact with Ireland and the north-western counties. Shropshire's ironworks were important sources of munitions. A letter written by the Royalist Sir Orlando Bridgeman in 1642-43 speaks of a ton of battery shot and a ton of grenades which had been made by Mathias Gervise at Leighton furnace.

In January 1642-43 Sir Francis Ottley invited the inhabitants of Shrewsbury to pledge themselves to support the king. The recruitment of Royalist forces continued. Richard Gough remembered that when he was about eight or nine, in 1642-43, Sir Paul Harris summoned the men of Pimhill hundred aged between 16 and 70 to assemble on Myddle Hill, where Robert More, brother of the rector of Myddle, stood by three or four pikes which had been struck into the ground, and offered 14 groats a week as wages for those who would serve the king. There was some disorder in the early months of the war as ill-disciplined soldiers, neither well-fed nor adequately paid, roamed the county. In October 1642 the Shrewsbury area was said to be full of troops who were constantly pretending to be quarrelling with Roundheads, but who were taking good bounty wherever they found it.

King Charles and Prince Rupert passed through Shropshire several times during the next three years. Twice during 1644 Prince Rupert assembled troops on Holloway Hill in Myddle parish before making rendezvous at Ellesmere. In the summer of that year he caused 13 Parliamentarian prisoners to be hanged in revenge for the execution by his opponents of 13 Irish soldiers. In June 1644 the king was in Shrewsbury during the campaign which led to the Battle of Cropredy Bridge in Oxfordshire. In May 1645 during the campaign which concluded with the royal defeat at Naseby, the

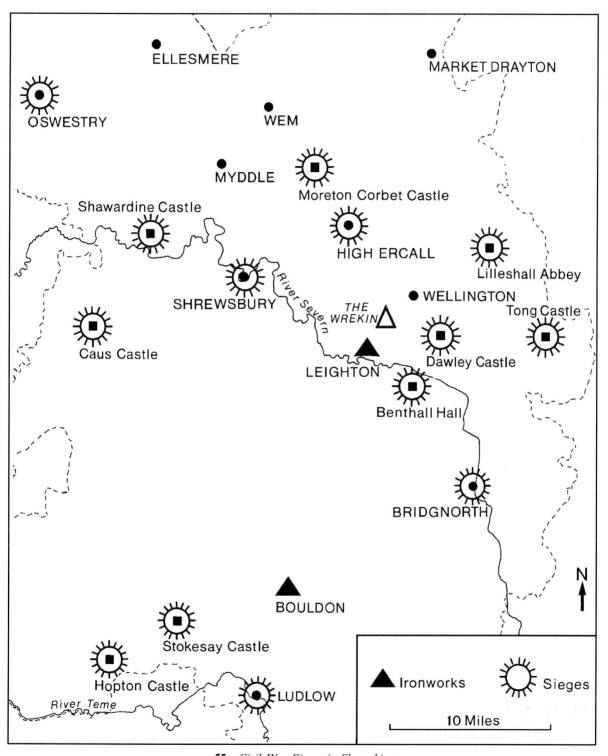

55 *Civil War Sieges in Shropshire*

56 The magnificent gatehouse of c.1620 at Stokesay Castle.

king was at Market Drayton and Prince Rupert at Newport. Charles twice passed through the county during the period between Naseby and his capture by the parliamentarian forces. In September 1645 he went from Raglan to Chester, taking care to avoid Shrewsbury and Oswestry, and on his return he visited the garrison at Bridgnorth.

There were few active Parliamentarians among the Shropshire gentry, but they included men of considerable ability, who against many odds brought the county under their control, and denied it to the Royalists as an area of safe passage and a source of munitions. In April 1643 the Parliamentarian Committee for Association for Warwickshire, Staffordshire and Shropshire was established, its members including Sir John Corbet, Richard More of Linley and Thomas Mytton of Halston. In August the Parliamentarians under Mytton, Humphrey Mackworth, Thomas Hunt and Richard Baxter established a garrison at Wem. Wem became the centre and symbol of the Parliamentary cause in Shropshire. Surrounded by an earthen rampart surmounted by a stout palisade of stakes from a coppice in the township of Lacon, the town stood like Luther's 'feste burg', a safe stronghold of the Protestant and Parliamentary cause, a little wooden citadel which was ultimately to bring about the subjugation of towns and castles of greater eminence.

The first significant Parliamentary success in Shropshire was the capture of Tong Castle by troops from Eccleshall on 28 December 1643, but their cause suffered a setback the following March when Royalists captured Hopton Castle which had been held by Parliamentarians from Brampton Bryan. Twenty-nine of the defenders, having refused quarter, were clubbed to death, according to normal military practice. In June 1644 the Parliamentarians captured Oswestry, which controlled several key routes into North Wales. Under the direction of the Royalist Colonel Edward Lloyd of Llanforda a new gate and drawbridge had been erected, the steeple of the parish church demolished, and the walls of the castle repaired. The garrison consisted almost entirely of Welshmen. After an attempt in January 1644 to lure Colonel Lloyd out of the town by the promise of a sumptuous meal, and an open attack in March 1644 which was repulsed, the town was taken by a small force under the Earl of Denbigh on 22 June 1644, at a time when the governor and part of the garrison had gone to Shrewsbury escorting prisoners. Denbigh captured 400 of the garrison, among them Sir Francis Newport. The fall of Oswestry was one of several events in the summer of 1644 which turned the tide of war against the king. The Royalists won the Battle of Cropredy Bridge in Oxfordshire, but on 3 July Prince Rupert was defeated at Marston Moor in Yorkshire.

The Royalist strongholds in Shropshire remained secure, but during 1645 the Parliamentarians gradually subdued them. Shrewsbury was captured early in the morning of 22 February 1644/5. The Parliamentarians from Wem had previously been repulsed on two sorties towards Shrewsbury, but they seem to have known that the garrison had been weakened by the dispatch of an expedition into Cheshire. The governor, Sir Michael Earnley, was unwell, and a stream of intelligence went from Parliamentarian

V *The church of St Peter, Myddle (SJ468235), of which Richard Gough, author of* The History of Myddle *was churchwarden.*

VI *The chapel in the grounds of Berwick House on the outskirts of Shrewbury (SJ47-3148), built in 1672 with a tower added* c.1731. *John Wesley preached in the chapel in 1769.*

VII *The Old Work at Wroxeter with an excavated hypocaust in the foreground (SJ565088).*

VIII *Attingham Park (SJ550099), designed by George Steuart, built in 1783-84, and later enlarged by John Nash. The mansion stands on the site of Tern Hall, an earlier house, and overlooks the site of Tern Works, the forge built by Abraham Darby I and his partners in 1710.*

sympathisers in the town to Wem. A group of carpenters approached the town in a small boat and cut down the stake fence between the castle and the Severn. Forty-two dismounted cavalry, and accompanied by a Puritan chaplain, stormed up the rampart below the Council House, while a body of infantry poured into the town through St Mary's Water Lane gate, where no resistance was offered. The Royalist guard in the Market Place was subdued and, once the North Gate had been occupied, the drawbridge was lowered to let in the main body of Parliamentarian cavalry. The governor was killed having refused quarter, after which the garrison surrendered on condition that its English members should be allowed to march to Ludlow, leaving the Irish as prisoners. Prince Maurice, who had arrived in Shrewsbury the previous day, was able to escape.

During the summer of 1645 the lesser Royalist garrisons were gradually mopped up. In the same month that Shrewsbury fell, a Parliamentarian force took Benthall Hall. The castles at Caus, Stokesay and Shrawardine fell in June, to be followed by Lilleshall Abbey and Dawley Castle in August, and Moreton Corbet Castle in September. On 21 March 1645/6 Bridgnorth was captured, many buildings being destroyed by a fire started by the retreating Royalists, and High Ercall was also taken. Finally Ludlow, the last significant Royalist stronghold, was captured by forces led by Sir William Brereton at the end of May.

King Charles I was executed on 30 January 1648/9, after which Royalists accepted his exiled son, later Charles II, as their king. He landed in Scotland, where on 1 January 1650/1 he was proclaimed king and called for support. His campaign ended with the Battle of Worcester on 3 September 1651 where he was decisively defeated by the New Model Army under Oliver Cromwell. He escaped northwards, reaching White Ladies Priory on the estates of the Roman Catholic Giffard family, and about a mile within Shropshire, at 3 a.m. on 4 September. The following day he set out for

57 *The leaning tower of Bridgnorth: the keep of the medieval castle after its partial destruction following the siege of the town during the Civil War (SO716926).*

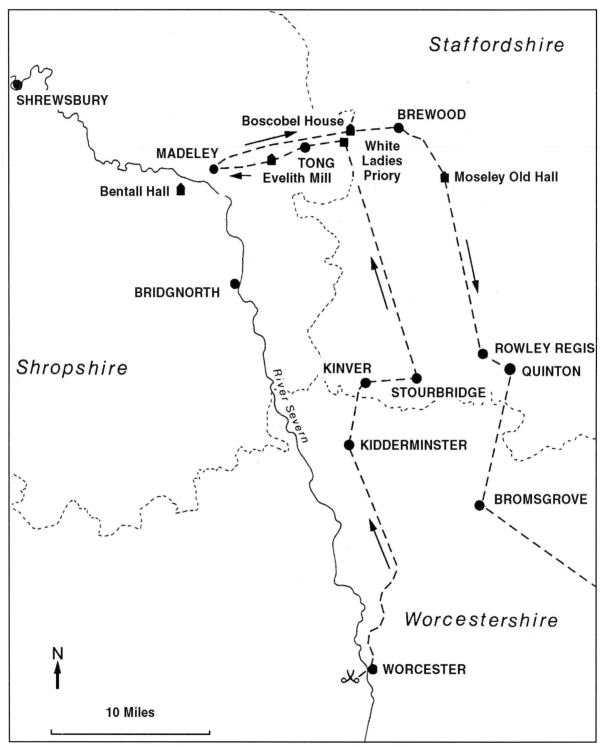

58 *The escape of Charles II after the Battle of Worcester.*

Wales in company with Richard Penderell, hoping to cross the Severn in the Gorge. They were challenged by the miller at Evelith, and spent the night in the barn of Francis Wolfe, master of the Coalbrookdale ironworks, at Upper House, Madeley. The Severn crossings were all guarded, so they returned to Boscobel, the main seat of the Giffards, which stands on the Shropshire/Staffordshire border in the heart of a wooded region. It was on 6 September that Charles hid in an oak tree while soldiers searched the surrounding woodlands. He headed southwards on 7 September, and sailed from Shoreham to France on 15 October.

59 *A medal commemorating the coronation of King Charles II depicting the oak tree in which he hid at Boscobel.*

After the fall of Ludlow the Parliamentary committee, first established in 1643, was reconstituted as a committee of assessment. Colonel John Benbow, who had played a distinguished rôle in the capture of Shrewsbury, was so appalled by the execution of the king that he rejoined the Royalist party. He was executed outside Shrewsbury Castle on 15 October 1651 as an example to other possible apostates. In the early 1650s many men of humble origins and radical opinions were appointed to the county committee and to the Commission of the Peace, but moderate men, and landowners like Lancelot Lee, Robert Corbet of Stanwardine and Edward Cresset of Cotes, continued to participate in the government of the county. Attempts to secure Shrewsbury Castle for the exiled king in 1654 and 1659 ended in failure.

The Civil War in Shropshire demonstrated how unused Englishmen had become to military ways. When a stretch of the walls of Shrewsbury was revealed in Roushill during building work in 1969, there was a marked contrast between the superb masonry of the 13th century and the clumsy patchings carried out in the 1640s. Just how the war affected Salopians is difficult to determine. For those trapped in the besieged towns of Shrewsbury, Oswestry and Bridgnorth it obviously caused shortages and brought the forcible quartering of troops. Many houses in the suburbs of Ludlow, particularly in Corve Street and Galdeford, were burned down, probably by Royalist defenders wanting to clear their lines of fire. The blockade of the Severn led to shortages of fuel and of imported groceries. In the countryside normal agricultural activities continued, subject to interruption by marauding soldiers of both sides. One tenant at Colemere was said in 1650 to have 'lost all by the warrs, not a ragg left'. Richard Gough recalled that 20 men from Myddle went to fight for the king and that 13 were killed. Long after the war, one of the few Myddle men who fought for parliament was to be seen going about the parish hobbling after a musket bullet passed through his leg. Gough concluded, 'if soe many dyed out of these 3 townes, wee may reasonable guesse that many thousands dyed in England in that warre'.

He was certainly correct, yet the war was a low-key affair compared with contemporary hostilities in continental Europe. Many strongholds were demolished after the war. The castles and walls of Oswestry and Bridgnorth were rendered indefensible. The castles of Dawley, Shrawardine and Caus became quarries for hardcore. It is some measure of the change which had come over Shropshire society between 1540 and 1650 that it should have proved itself so unmilitaristic in the Civil War.

11

Salopian Goods and Chattels

The study of probate inventories during the last two decades has vastly enlarged our understanding of 17th- and 18th-century Shropshire. A probate inventory is a list of a person's possessions, excluding his landed property, made after his death. An inventory had to be produced in a church court before probate of a will or a bond of administration could be granted. Important new evidence on many aspects of the county's history has been discovered. Only a little work has yet been done on inventories from before the Civil War, although many survive for the parishes within Lichfield diocese. Few inventories are available for the period after 1760, although some survive from the Peculiar Court of Bridgnorth from the very end of the 18th century. Serious work, involving the full transcription and analysis of inventories, has been completed or is in progress in the Telford area, in Leighton, in Newport and Edgmond, Shifnal, Shrewsbury, Bridgnorth, Ludlow, the Clee Hills region, Richards Castle, Ellesmere, the borough of Wenlock and the parishes around Bishop's Castle.

Inventories give a vivid picture of agriculture in the late 17th and early 18th centuries. In the parishes in the north of Telford they show that the use of oxen as draught beasts was diminishing in the first half of the 18th century, that rye was falling into disfavour as a crop, that new crops like clover were being grown, and that the size of cattle herds was increasing by the 1740s after a period of decline at the beginning of the century. The parishes of Wrockwardine and Lilleshall formed the southern edge of the Cheshire cheese region and numerous inventories describe well-equipped dairy farms, with relatively large milking herds, producing cheese as a cash product within a mixed farming economy. Richard Shelton of Lilleshall who died in 1683 left 13 milking cows and 210 cheeses worth £8. Dairy farming was particularly prosperous in the parish of Adderley which lies on the Cheshire border north of Market Drayton. Ninety-three inventories made between 1660 and 1750 survive for inhabitants of Adderley. Of those, 60 had herds of cows, the mean size of which was 23, a much higher average than for most Shropshire parishes. By contrast only 12 had flocks of sheep. Cheese to the value of £20 or over (approximately one ton) was listed on the inventories of no less than 17 Adderley farmers. Richard Furber of Adderley, who died in 1660, had 137 cattle in his dairy herd, apart from his draught oxen, and cheese worth £168, probably weighing about eight tons, in his house. William Tankard who died in 1695 had 50 cattle and four tons of cheese worth £80.

60 *A pestle and mortar.*

Farming in the Coalbrookdale coalfield was generally on a smaller scale, and in the south of the area a high proportion of the population had no contact with agriculture. Work in parishes between Shifnal and the Severn suggests the existence of a sheep/corn pattern of farming with numerous flocks of sheep, generally much larger than the flocks in Wrockwardine and Lilleshall. Edward Fregleton of Claverley who died just after the 1693 harvest had been gathered in had grain worth £150, as well as hay and clover worth £30 and 80 strikes of malt. A herd of 25 dairy cattle provided the milk to make the 30 pounds of butter and the 80 cheeses in his store chamber, but his arable fields were manured by his flock of 240 sheep. William Crowther of Beobridge, Claverley, who died in November 1760, was one of the first Shropshire agriculturalists to be described as a 'farmer' rather than a 'husbandman', 'yeoman' or 'gent'. He owned grain worth more than £50 in his barns, a crop of winter corn valued at £10 and 180 sheep worth £54.

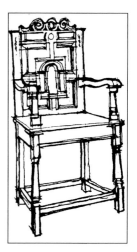

61 *A wainscot chair made in 1662 by the Shrewsbury joiner Richard Ellis for the guild hall of the Drapers' Company.*

In Stottesdon in the fertile Rea Valley there were large mixed farms, with dairy herds from whose milk cheese was manufactured as a cash product. Humphrey Bromley of Wallfurlong, who died in 1681, ploughed with six oxen, and grew dredge (a mixture of wheat and rye) which was probably his bread corn, and barley for brewing. He had 23 beasts in his dairy herd, and a cheese chamber in which 17 cheeses were stacked on ten shelves. His six pigs probably lived on skimmed milk. The inventories of Richards Castle often quote acreages of crops, which rarely happens elsewhere in Shropshire. Turnips are listed on four inventories between 1684 and 1726. Anne Cooke, a widow whose inventory was taken in 1690, had a dairy herd of 12 beasts, kept 44 sheep and two pigs, ploughed with horses and was growing five acres of 'corn and wheat', four acres of oats, eight acres of 'oats and barley', four acres of lent grain (probably spring-sown barley) and two acres of turnips in the Vallets, a field which is still regarded as good ground for root crops. Several Richards Castle inventories list apples and many more include cider presses or mills. In the Bishop's Castle area it seems that practices like ploughing with oxen persisted longer than in the east of the county. There were some farms with large flocks of sheep as well as substantial dairy herds. John Bason of Bishop's Castle who died in 1739 had a flock of 700 sheep, he ploughed with 12 oxen, and had a dairy herd of 42 beasts. Wool stored in his house was worth £24, and his stock of cheese and butter was valued at £10.

Inventories show that in almost every part of Shropshire flax and hemp were grown in closes adjacent to farmhouses and cottages. The crops were retted, scutched with tewtaws, combed with heckles, and spun into yarn in the homes of the growers, after which the yarn was taken to professional weavers to be made into cloth for use as bed or table linen.

Inventories also provide much information about towns. Mercers sold almost every product that was brought into the county. Most had ranges of woollen and linen fabrics, each made in a part of Britain which specialised in its manufacture, or imported from abroad. They sold hosiery and haberdashery, and imported groceries like sugar, spices and dried fruit.

62 *Scales.*

They sold paper and printed books, tar and pitch, salted herrings, soap, candles, which some of them manufactured, and tobacco which many of them processed. Mercers in the larger towns began to specialise as dealers in fabrics, tobacconists, grocers or tallow chandlers in the 18th century. Alexander Wood of Oswestry who died in 1700 was a grocer, and had most of the stocks normally held by a mercer, with the exception of textiles. Several apothecaries' inventories have been found, among them that of John Wilkes of Newport, who died in 1686. His stock included electuaries, cordials, purgatives, syrups, rhubarb and senna. Several detailed inventories of tanners survive. Shoemakers' inventories are numerous and normally of rather low value with little stock and a minimum of equipment. Glovers worked in most towns, and usually dressed their own leather. Saddlers were among the wealthiest tradesmen. Humphrey Castleton of Shifnal who died in 1665 left goods worth £361, including many semi-finished products in his two shops at Shifnal and Wellington.

In most Shropshire towns there were blacksmiths, coopers, hatters, tailors, butchers and bakers, while candlesticks were made by brasiers and pewterers, of whom there was a concentration in Newport. Richard Plummer, pewterer of Ludlow who died in 1682, left possessions worth £417, including kettles, pans and sad (or flat) ware in pewter, candlesticks and pots in brass, his moulds and other equipment, and stocks of pottery, Burslem, Clee Hill and Dutch ware, which he was selling. Richard Kempster, tin plate worker of Bridgnorth, who died in 1756, made an astonishing range of products, tea canisters, lanthorns, teakettles, brawn tins and japanned quart measures.

Many inventories relate to the building trade. Caleb Higgins of Shifnal, who died in 1727, was a glazier whose possessions included vices, diamonds, lead, suckers, dividers and Bristol squares of glass. Isaac Lloyd, a Shrewsbury carpenter who died in 1664, was apparently engaged on a contract at the castle where he left 'ropes, pulleys and other engines'.

Dyers have been identified in most Shropshire towns, and the inventories of those from Wellington have been used to explain the range of processes which they were using. In Shrewsbury numerous inventories show that the shearmen were as poor in fact as they were by reputation. Moses Law of Bridgnorth who died in 1712 operated what was virtually a proto-factory. He had large stocks of wool with equipment for carding, weaving, dyeing and finishing it. His finished woollen cloth was worth more than £500.

In Shrewsbury, Bridgnorth and Ludlow the inventories of several luxury tradesmen have been discovered. Joseph Wayman, perukemaker of Ludlow, who died in 1748, had razors, periwig ribbons and curling pipes for carrying on his occupation, while Thomas Holland, sword cutler of Shrewsbury who died in 1689, made a range of mundane objects like shoemakers' knives and scissors, as well as swords with silver hilts and boxes with fish skin decorations.

William Fosbrook of Claverley who died in 1731 was a papermaker, and his inventory lists paper moulds and frames felts, shears and 18 cwt of rags, which were worth the surprisingly large sum of £11 14s., as well as quantities of paper at different stages of production. He seems to have supplied papers to merchants in Stafford, Worcester, Birmingham and Dublin. John Higgins was a rural tanner working on the county boundary at Richards Castle in premises still called the Tanhouse. His stock of leather was worth £231, and he had waste leather, horns and hair worth over £12, and a mill for grinding the oak bark used in the tanning process. Thomas Sandford, who died in 1726, occupied an oil mill at Sandford in the parish of Prees, where, in addition to iron tools, a weigh beam, and a stock of barrels, he had over 400 gallons of linseed oil worth more than £50.

A detailed picture is emerging of changes in Shropshire households between 1660 and 1760, a period when standards of comfort were improving and new luxuries were being introduced. In North Telford it has been shown that while in the 1660s most people had only one change of sheets for each of their beds, by the 1700s there were three pairs per bed, and that the number increased in subsequent decades, when well-stocked linen chests came to be regarded as a kind of accumulated capital. Seventeenth-century inventories show surprisingly little pottery, most of the tableware being made of pewter or wood. Pottery became more common during the first half of the 18th century, and did so at an accelerating rate after 1750. Pewter and brass ware were found in almost every household. By the 1730s many people had more than was needed for everyday use and displayed it on dressers, items of furniture unknown in the 17th century but found frequently by the 1740s. Looking glasses became more common between 1700 and 1750, and Salopians' conceptions of time were being revolutionised by an increased use of clocks. In North Telford only seven clocks are recorded in 357 inventories between 1660 and 1700, but 80 are listed in 489 inventories between 1700 and 1750, during which period the mean value of clocks fell from £3 10s. 0d. to £1 15s. 0d. Table cutlery was used only in the homes of the wealthy before 1750, but became relatively common afterwards. Home brewing was widespread, and many people who kept only one or two cows made their own butter and cheese. The mention of a grate on an inventory implies the use of coal as the household fuel. Virtually every household in the Coalbrookdale coalfield and Bridgnorth used coal, but in Bishop's Castle, a place remote from any source of coal, its use was rare although increasing between 1700 and 1750, and in the surrounding rural parishes it was not used at all.

63 *Fragments of tea and coffee pots of the first half of the 18th century found on waste tips in Jackfield during investigations in the early 1980s by the Ironbridge Institute. Archaeological evidence that tea and coffee pots were being made in Shropshire supports the evidence in probate inventories that tea and coffee drinking greatly increased between 1710 and 1760.*

Some inventories and wills provide information about clothing. William Hills, apparently an old man, who died in Shrewsbury in 1667, had garments worth about £6, including a suit and cloak, one pair of black and two of grey hose, a satin cap and a purple gown. The wardrobe of Jane Little of the Moor, Richards Castle, who died in 1693, included a purple Indian crepe night gown, a dark-coloured shawl flowered at the ends with red and green, and a black-striped satin gown and petticoat.

Lists of what dead people owned might seem too far removed from the world of real events to be of real value as historical evidence. Yet the more work is done on inventories the more they seem to relate to the real world. The inventory of Joshua Johnson, a Wellington mercer, made in 1695, has stocks of most goods but a pathetically small quantity of sugar, compared with that of other mercers, something which is probably explained by the chaos in the sugar trade caused by the wars with France and a succession of hurricanes. Johnson's spices were particularly expensive, but again, 1695 was a year in which prices generally were high, owing to the effects of war. The inventory is a reminder that what citizens in a small market town could buy was directly affected by world events. Edward Caldwall, vicar of Stottesdon, who died in 1687, left books worth £52 19s. 5d. and £18 in cash, both exceptionally high figures. His appraisers included Thomas Wickstead, stationer and bookseller of Bridgnorth, from which it may be inferred that his books were priced accurately, and the inventory was taken on 5 April just after his cash in hand had been augmented by Easter offerings. The inventory which most vividly reflects contemporary events is that of Walter Astley of Newport taken in 1666. His appraisers listed goods which were 'the residue and remainder ... wch are now left undestroyed by ye late ruines of fire wch hapned in Newport', and they included 'part of his Cloathes & weareing aparell and ye rest Burnt'. On 16 May 1665, 162 houses were destroyed by fire in Newport. Inventories, particularly if used in large numbers, offer many insights into the world of real events.

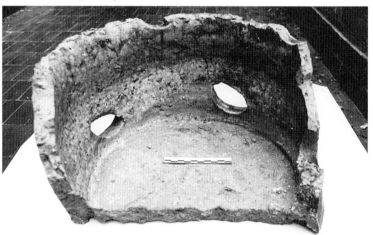

64   *A sagger for making salt-glaze pottery found during archaeological investigation of waste tips in the Ironbridge Gorge in the early 1980s.*

12

County Society in the 18th Century

Eighteenth-century Shropshire was a community in which power was shared and sometimes contested between the squirearchy, who were the resident owners of estates of modest size, and the major gentry who held a higher proportion of the land in Shropshire than in any other county. By 1700 Shrewsbury was one of the principal provincial cities, a social centre for the gentry of the county and for many from North Wales. Celia Fiennes noted that 'there are abundance of people of quality lives in Shrewsbury, more than in any town except Nottingham', and the atmosphere of the town is acutely observed in George Farquhar's *The Recruiting Officer*, written in 1706. Many county families had houses in central Shrewsbury, and the town provided professional men and specialised craftsmen for the needs of the wealthy. Ludlow became a social centre on a lesser scale for the gentry of South Shropshire and North Herefordshire.

65 *The centre of Ludlow, 1808.*

The groupings within the upper ranks of Shropshire society were revealed in the pattern of politics within the county. The Lieutenancy was held by the Whig gentry families, with one short break, but the Quarter Sessions were largely controlled by the Tory squires. In parliamentary politics, the squires controlled the two prestigious county seats, leaving the majority of the ten borough seats to the Whig gentry. Sir John Astley, after a period as MP for Shrewsbury between 1727 and 1734, sat for the county for 38 years from 1734 until his death in 1772. Richard Lyster of Rowton was elected for Shrewsbury in 1732 but lost his seat when it was ruled that residents in Abbey Foregate were not entitled to vote in Shrewsbury elections. He was elected for the county in 1740 and remained its representative until he died in 1766. Lyster's eloquent epitaph, inscribed on a memorial designed by T.F. Pritchard, paid tribute to his unshaken integrity, tried honour, unwearied attention and steady attachment to the true interest of his country, and to his work as a magistrate and churchman. It recalled that 'his house, like his heart, was open to his friends and more a model of ancient than of modern hospitality'.

Contested elections were expensive, and the poll of 1737 was the last for 94 years for the county seats. In the early years of the century the most powerful political figure in the county was Henry Newport, third Earl of Bradford. On his death in 1734 the inheritance was complex, and no one individual within his family retained his influence. Bradford's political successor was H.A. Herbert of Oakly Park, who became Lord Lieutenant

66 *The gazebo designed by Thomas Farnolls Pritchard in the garden of No. 27 Broad Street, Ludlow (SO513743), which uses circle and ogee decorative motifs, similar to those employed by Pritchard in the design of the Iron Bridge.*

in 1735, and gained the lapsed titles of Lord Herbert of Chirbury in 1743 and Earl of Powis in 1748. In the 1750s he was the acknowledged leader of the 'Shropshire Whigs', a group of gentry MPs who met in London before each parliamentary session. Powis obtained government appointments, military promotions and other marks of favour for the group and their families. He did not normally interfere in Shrewsbury's affairs, but when, in 1749, he attempted to nominate a master of the House of Correction, an opponent complained 'Lord Powis is more absolute in this part of the world than the King of France is in his capital city'. In the political confusion which followed the accession of George III in 1760, Powis lost the Lieutenancy to William Pulteney, Earl of Bath, the inheritor by circuitous means of some the lands of the Newport Earls of Bradford, but he regained it on Bath's death in 1764, and held it until his own death in 1772, when he was succeeded by a new and powerful figure in the county's politics.

Robert Clive was born at Styche Hall, Moreton Say, in 1725, a member of a respected family of minor gentry. He went to Madras to work as a clerk with the East India Company in 1742, and returned to England, for only the second time, in 1760 as governor of the Company's possessions in Bengal, and the much-lauded victor of the Battle of Plassey. The Earl of Powis immediately introduced him to the Corporation of Shrewsbury, and he became MP for the town. Clive clearly intended to build up political influence in the county. From 1763 he was formally allied with the Earl of Powis, who regarded him as his successor. In 1763 Clive purchased the Walcot estate and with it electoral influence at Bishop's Castle, which ceased to be a pliant borough, available at any election to the highest bidder, although Clive and his successors could only control it by the expenditure of much energy and money. In June 1771 Clive purchased Oakly Park from the Earl of Powis who died the following year. Clive succeeded him to the Lord Lieutenancy, but his health had suffered during his last spell in India in 1765-66. He took his own life in 1774. The second Lord Clive married the sister of the second Earl of Powis in 1784 and, when the Earl died unmarried in 1801, his estates passed to his brother-in-law, for whom the title Earl of Powis was re-created in 1804. The Lieutenancy remained in the family until 1839, and through the control of Ludlow and Bishop's Castle the Herbert-Clives remained a powerful force in Shropshire politics.

The Shropshire borough electorates were relatively large and each constituency had to be nursed by its patrons. Bridgnorth was under the influence of the Whitmores of Apley Park, at least one of whom was returned for the town at every election between the Restoration and 1870, with the exception of that of 1710. The saying grew up 'All on one side like a Bridgnorth election', but even in Bridgnorth, popular opinion, particularly on the choice of second members, had to be taken into account. A similar situation prevailed in the borough of Wenlock, where the influence of the Forester family was predominant. Shrewsbury was the most fiercely contested of the boroughs. The electorate was large and the rights of burgesses to vote were subject to dispute. Thomas Hill of Hawkstone was one MP for the town, and from 1760 his companion was Robert Clive, but the domination of this Whig faction was challenged by the Bath family. Part of the estate of Henry Newport, third Earl of Bradford, had passed to his bastard son, John Newport, on whose decease it devolved to William Pulteney, Earl of Bath, 'a brilliant, eloquent, vindictive, mean man', who succeeded the Earl of Powis as Lord Lieutenant in 1760. In 1761 he attempted to secure his son's election for Shrewsbury. On Bath's death in 1764 the inheritance passed to his brother, who died in 1767, whereupon it went to his cousin's daughter, the wife of a lowland Scot, William Johnson, who took the name of Pulteney. In the election of 1768 Pulteney challenged the Whigs for one of the Shrewsbury seats, and mounted a serious campaign in the election of 1774, which he lost. He contested the result and was returned in place of one of the victorious Whigs. Meanwhile Robert Clive had committed suicide, and in the by-election which followed early in 1775 Pulteney gained control of the second seat by securing the election of his nominee John Corbet. Pulteney remained MP for Shrewsbury until his death in 1805, but there was much rivalry for the other seat, which reached its height in 1796 when there was a contest between the Hawkstone and Attingham branches of the Hill family, in which the latter, the losers, spent £15,414.

One of the most influential figures in county society in the mid-18th century was a lawyer, John Ashby, the 'guardian of many secrets', who was town clerk of Shrewsbury, three times deputy sheriff, agent to the Clives and political agent to the Foresters of Willey. Ashby co-ordinated parliamentary lobbying on turnpike roads, and built the *Lion Hotel* next to his own house on Wyle Cop, where he provided a magnificent assembly room,

67 *The country house in Gothic—Longner Hall, by John Nash, built in 1803-4.*

68 *George Steuart's portico at Attingham, built in 1783-85.*

'to promote the general good of this town and county'. When the contents of the *Lion* were sold after his death, the sale notice announced that he had stocked the cellar 'with a large assortment of excellent wines and liquors, to which since his decease has been added the stock of his own private cellar, which was considerable'.

Many of Shropshire's notable country houses date from the 18th century. The leading architect of the first half of the century was Francis Smith of Warwick, who worked at Davenport, Kinlet, Berwick, Buntingsdale, Mawley Hall and Beaumaris House in Newport. The most interesting architect of the middle decades was Thomas Farnolls Pritchard, who was born in 1723, the son of a Shrewsbury joiner whose occupation he followed. He designed the Foundling Hospital in Shrewsbury (now part of Shrewsbury School), Swan Hill Court, which was intended as a town house to further the ambitions of the Earl of Bath, and Hatton Grange, Shifnal. He refurbished older town and country houses, among them Shipton Hall, built in 1587, to which he gave a Gothic rear elevation and a magnificent interior. He added to No. 27 Broad Street, Ludlow a characteristic frontage with a heavily emphasised central bay, and a delightful Gothic gazebo, and gave a subtle new interior and a striking Gothic doorcase to Ludlow's Guildhall. He also designed church monuments, notable examples of which survive at Acton Round, Cound and Alberbury.

Pritchard assembled a team of skilled craftsmen, the wood and stone carver, John Nelson, the plasterer Joseph Bromfield, and the sculptor Alexander van der Hagen, who carried on the traditions he had established after his death. About 1770 Pritchard left his workshop on Pride Hill, moved to a turret house at Eyton on Severn, the remnant of the great 17th-century mansion of the Newport family, and became more concerned with bridges. He had been involved as a surveyor in the replacement of the English Bridge in Shrewsbury in the 1760s, and of Atcham Bridge in the 1770s, but in both cases designs by John Gwynn were actually used. He was surveyor in 1772 for a bridge over the Teme at Bringewood Forge, and designed the bridge over the Severn at the new canal town of Stourport in 1773-75. It was Pritchard who suggested the building of an iron bridge across the Severn near Coalbrookdale in 1773. The project was aided by John Wilkinson and carried through by Abraham Darby III. Legal difficulties impeded progress after an Act of Parliament had been obtained in 1776, and at the time of Pritchard's death on 21 December 1777 work on the ground had only begun. Nevertheless the ogee and circle ornamentation of the bridge, similar to the decorations on the Ludlow gazebo, served as Pritchard's signature. Much of Pritchard's work is characterised by richly ornamented plasterwork and woodwork, sometimes with Gothic motifs and sometimes with 'bamboo' columns.

During Pritchard's lifetime the profession of architect became established in Shropshire. On the death of Alexander van der Hagen in 1791, his business was taken over by the stone masons John Carline and John Tilley. Their works included the Welsh Bridge and Claremont Buildings. The Haycock family secured contracts for several public buildings, including the county gaol, the Shirehall and the *Tontine Hotel* at Ironbridge. In 1786 or 1787 William Pulteney brought to Shrewsbury the ambitious young Scot Thomas Telford, who was welcomed as a man whose ability and frugal habits lifted him above the corrupting tangle of local connections. Telford's first job was to remodel the Castle, but from 1788 he was employed as surveyor for the county. In the course of this appointment which lasted till his death in 1834 he built 42 county bridges. He designed St Mary's church at Bridgnorth, St Michael, Madeley, and St Leonard, Malins Lee, as well as Kingsland House in Shrewsbury. From 1793 he was concerned with canals. He had several able protégés. John Simpson, a Scots mason, worked with him from 1793 until he died in 1815. Matthew Davidson, also a stone mason, executed the stonework for many of his great bridges. William Hazledine, born and bred in the Shropshire charcoal iron trade, established a foundry in Coleham in Shrewsbury in the mid-1790s, set up an ironworks at Plas Kynaston near Wrexham, and acquired forges in the Tern valley, a furnace complex in the Ironbridge Gorge and mines in the Coalbrookdale Coalfield. He provided the iron for the Chirk and Pontcysyllte aqueducts and for many of Telford's bridges. He gained a great fortune, acquired much property in Shrewsbury, and was one of the town's most influential citizens at the time of his death in 1840.

The rôle of county government assumed more importance in the late 18th century. Telford oversaw the completion of a new county gaol on Castle Hill in Shrewsbury, which had been designed by the architect J.H. Haycock. It followed principles laid down by the prison reformer John Howard who visited Shrewsbury several times in the mid-1770s and again on 10 December 1788 when the building was almost complete. Ten years later a bust of Howard by J. Bacon RA was placed over the entrance. In 1784-86 a new Shirehall designed by John Hiram Haycock was built in the

69 *The most popular early view of the Iron Bridge, engraved by William Ellis, from an original painting by Michaelangelo Rooker, which was commissioned by the bridge proprietors.*

70   *The entrance lodge of Shrewsbury Gaol (SJ495130), completed in 1793. The lodge was probably designed by Thomas Telford. The bust in the niche is of the prison reformer John Howard who visited Shrewsbury while the gaol was being built in 1788. Until the 1840s public executions took place on the roof of the left-hand bay.*

71   *Lifting bridges near Moss Farm, Whixall, on the Prees branch of the Ellesmere Canal (SJ492346).*

Square, and the course of High Street was straightened as part of the same project. The foundations of the building proved inadequate, partly because it was on the line of an ancient watercourse, and in 1833-37 it was rebuilt by Sir Robert Smirke.

In many respects Shropshire became a more integrated community during the 18th century. The Salop Infirmary, founded in 1745, was intended to cater for the whole county. Its annual meetings were held on the Friday of race week. The two regiments of foot which in 1881 became the King's Shropshire Light Infantry, were both founded in the mid-18th century, the 53rd by William Whitmore of Apley in 1755-56, and the 85th by William, Viscount Pulteney, son of the Earl of Bath, in 1759. Another unifying factor was the establishment of the county's first newspaper, the *Shrewsbury Chronicle*, in 1772. By 1800 landowners were increasingly co-operating over agricultural improvement. Among the acts for enclosing open commons passed in the last two decades of the century were those for the wetlands in Kinnerley and Melverley in 1786, the sandy heaths around Prees and Moreton Say in 1795, and for the uplands of the Long Mynd in 1788. Landowners also brought parishes into unions for the administration of the Poor Law. The parishes in Shrewsbury united in 1784, those around Oswestry and Ellesmere in 1791, and those in the Whitchurch area and around Shrewsbury (the later Atcham Poor Law Union) in 1792. The Montgomery and Pool Union, with its workhouse at Forden, was also established in 1792 and included the Shropshire parishes of Worthen and Chirbury.

For a few years at the end of the 18th century a score or so men of unusual ability were active in Shropshire. The group included William Hazledine, Thomas Telford, the Rev. Hugh Owen, author of *Some Account of the Ancient and Present State of Shrewsbury*, Dr. Samuel Butler, headmaster of Shrewsbury School from 1798-1836, who restored its academic reputation and increased the number of scholars from about twenty in 1798 to 295 by 1832, and Charles Bage, designer of the Ditherington and Castlefields flax mills, mayor of Shrewsbury and one of the founders of the town's Lancasterian School. The group was linked with the entrepreneurs of the Coalbrookdale Coalfield, particularly with William Reynolds. Canal-building brought them into contact with gentry like Thomas Eyton, who reputedly suggested the construction of the iron aqueduct at Longdon, and Rowland Hunt of Boreatton, one of the promoters of the Ellesmere Canal, who 'with constant and unwearied zeal employed the talents committed to him in promoting everything that was beneficial to the community and county in which he resided'. Many of the group came together at Longnor Hall, the home of Archdeacon Joseph Plymley, author of *A General View of the Agriculture of Shropshire*, published in 1802, to which some of them contributed. Plymley was active in the anti-Slavery movement, through which he had contacts with William and Richard Reynolds, and with Telford's friend Archibald Alison, curate of Kenley, philosopher, and author of an *Essay on Taste*. Shared intellectual interests brought together Anglican land-owners like Eyton, Hunt and Plymley with Shrewsbury's dissenting élite. One member of this élite was Robert Waring Darwin who had set up in practice as a physician in Shrewsbury in 1786, and built a new house, *The Mount*, ten years later. It was there on 12 February 1809 that his son Charles was born. By the time he was eight, Charles Darwin had developed an enthusiasm for collecting plants, shells and minerals. The scientific study of geology was one of the passions of the leading figures in the Shropshire enlightenment, and it proved a lasting influence on the author of *The Origin of Species*.

72 *The wooden bridge at Coalport.*

73 *Longnor Hall, home of the Rev. Joseph Plymley and his diarist sister Katherine, and chief meeting place of the leaders of the 'Shropshire enlightenment'.*

13

The Evangelical Revival

Between the 1730s and the mid-19th century there was a quickening of religious activity in Britain, a proliferation of new denominations, a new awareness of theological issues and an increased level of attendance at church services. The history of religion in Shropshire during this period follows national trends, but it is of particular interest because several figures of national standing were active in the county, and because Shropshire had many idiosyncratic groups.

A division between the established church and those unable to accept its tenets was institutionalised after the Restoration of Charles II in 1660. Many clergy were ejected from their livings in 1662 and, when the Declaration of Indulgence of 1672 allowed the registration of dissenting places of worship, 57 were recorded in Shropshire. Seven were in Shrewsbury and many others in the larger towns, but some were in the deepest depths of the countryside at places like Cold Weston, Acton Round and More. Quakers established meetings in Shrewsbury in the 1650s and at Broseley in the 1690s. Dissenting congregations had their own chapels in most Shropshire towns by the mid-18th century.

74 *Herring-bone masonry in the wall of All Saints', Culmington.*

The first indications of a new religious awakening in Shropshire came in the 1730s. They may have been stimulated by the spells of high mortality in the West Midlands in the 1720s and in 1739-41 which are evident in every parish register. Before 1732 a group of pious people began to meet regularly in Ludlow, sometimes assembling at Huck's Barn in Richards Castle. They subsequently built a meeting house, but for about two years they had 'no constant supply but what came by providence'. In Broseley a chapel was built in February 1741-42, which for two years had 'no constant supply but what by the providence of God ministers of other congregations were sometimes sent to assist us'. The meeting developed into a Baptist society, which, like the church in Ludlow, had links with Christians in Leominster, a town where the fires of the Evangelical Revival burned particularly strongly. There was a congregation of Methodists in Shrewsbury from about 1744, although it was another 17 years before John Wesley, the founder of Methodism, visited the town, and the society owed its later strength to Thomas Brocas, gardener at Whitehall, a local preacher who was active in the 1780s.

The most important figure in the Evangelical Revival in Shropshire, one of the Revival's most profound thinkers and perhaps its saintliest man,

was John Fletcher (otherwise Jean Guillaume de la Fléchère), vicar of Madeley from 1760 to 1785. Fletcher was born on the shores of Lake Geneva in 1729, and in 1752 became tutor to the sons of Thomas Hill of Tern Hall, Atcham. After experiencing conversion, he had contacts with John and Charles Wesley, and was ordained as a priest within the Church of England. In 1760 he accepted the living of Madeley, perhaps because he appreciated the industrial changes which were taking place in the district, and wished to confront the problems which they brought about. The language of his sermons and other publications reveals a concern with the sudden deaths in local pits, with the blinding horrors of flame-filled ironworks and the brutal drudgery of the work of bow-haulers on the Severn. John Wesley visited Fletcher at Madeley in 1764 and on several occasions afterwards, and saw him as his successor as leader of the connexion which he had built up, but Fletcher preferred to avoid involvement in national affairs. Ill health forced him to spend five months abroad in 1770 and between 1777 and 1781 he was in his native Switzerland. On his return he married Mary Bosanquet. He died in 1785, but until her own death in 1815 Mary Fletcher maintained much of his work. She lived in the Vicarage, and collaborated with the church authorities and with Wesleyan Methodist ministers. The meetings she ran were carried on through the 1820s by her adopted daughter

75 *Thomas Telford's church of St Michael, Madeley, completed in 1797 (SJ670045). To the left of the church is Madeley Vicarage, which at the time the drawing was made was the home of Mary, widow of the Rev. John Fletcher, and the Vicarage Barn where she led services.*

Mary Tooth, and close links continued between the Church and the Wesleyans in Madeley until a Wesleyan chapel was built in 1833. Fletcher's holiness impressed all who met him. One of his friends called him 'the greatest man that has lived in this century'.

After Fletcher's death the Methodist societies in Shropshire gradually established themselves as part of the Wesleyan Connexion. John Wesley formed a short-lived Shrewsbury Circuit in 1765, which was revived in 1792, after which the numbers of Wesleyans in the county grew rapidly, and circuits proliferated. Wesleyan Methodism was strong in the coalfield and in most towns, but relatively weak in the countryside. During a revival in the coalfield in 1821 Primitive Methodist preachers arrived in Wrockwardine Wood and Revivalists in Dawley. Primitive Methodism had been born in the Potteries in 1807 when a group of Wesleyans insisted on holding large open-air camp meetings. One such meeting, an isolated occurrence, took place on the Wrekin in 1808. The Primitive Methodists from Tunstall who arrived in the coalfield in 1821 were part of a three-pronged advance into Shropshire. From Wrockwardine Wood, where they built the first Primitive chapel in the county, they moved to Shrewsbury and thence to Bishop's Castle and Clun. Missionaries from Burland in Cheshire crossed the border in 1822 to Prees Green from where they spread across the whole of North

76   Wrockwardine Wood Primitive Methodist church (SJ70-1123) rebuilt in 1864 incorporating the first Primitive Methodist church in Shropshire, erected on the site in 1822, the dedication stone of which can be seen on the side of the building beneath the eaves to the left of the window in the second bay.

Shropshire. In 1823 missionaries from Darlaston established the Hopton Bank circuit in one of the wildest areas of squatter settlement on the Clee Hills, and subsequently took Primitive Methodism to Ludlow and Leintwardine. Throughout rural Shropshire the Primitives were the most numerous Nonconformist denomination in the 19th century. The Revivalists who arrived in Dawley in 1821 affiliated in 1829 to the Methodist New Connexion, which also established a Shrewsbury circuit in the 1830s, and absorbed another group of schismatic Methodists in Oswestry in the 1840s. The Overton (Flintshire) circuit of the Wesleyan Methodist Association opened chapels in the Oswestry area. In the Coalbrookdale Coalfield and in Shrewsbury congregations of Reformers who split from the Wesleyans in the early 1850s became part of the United Methodist Free Church in 1857. Congregations of Calvinistic Methodists (now the Presbyterian Church of Wales) met in Oswestry and Shrewsbury.

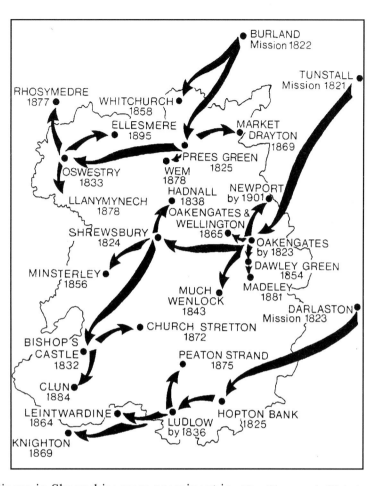

77 *The spread of Primitive Methodism across Shropshire.*

Apart from Fletcher, other Anglicans in Shropshire were prominent in the Evangelical Revival. The two sons of Sir Rowland Hill of Hawkstone, who died in 1783, both achieved some national fame. Richard, the elder, was a lay preacher, and in 1770 was the antagonist of Fletcher in the theological dispute known as the Calvinist Controversy. He was MP for Shrewsbury from 1776 to 1806, and espoused such Evangelical causes as Sunday observance and opposition to bull-baiting. His brother Rowland became famous as a preacher at the Surrey Chapel in London which opened in 1783. Edward Stillingfleet, vicar of Shawbury from 1768 to 1776, and Edward de Courcy his curate, who was vicar of St Alkmund's, Shrewsbury from 1774 until 1803, were well known for their Evangelicalism.

There was a quickening of activity among the older dissenting denominations in the late 18th century. Several congregations tended towards Unitarianism, which caused a schism in the old-established High Street congregation in Shrewsbury, as a result of which its minister Job Orton led a group who rejected the new ideas to form a church on Swan Hill in 1766. In 1796 the Independents (or Congregationalists) formed a county-wide association of churches, which had 15 affiliated congregations by 1811 and

33 in 1823. Six Baptist churches formed a similar organisation in 1808, which by 1824 incorporated 13 congregations. Many dissenters travelled long distances to find congenial ministers. Samuel Hughes, a lead miner born in 1809 who lived in Crows Nest Dingle, Snailbeach, helped to build the nearby Lord's Hill Chapel, but thought the chapel's minister lacked inspiration, and became a 'speckled bird', seeking satisfying preaching in Shrewsbury, Broseley and Little London near Wolverhampton.

Quakerism in Shropshire became largely concentrated in the coalfield under the leadership of the Darby and Reynolds families of Coalbrookdale and Ketley, who had contacts with leading Quakers from other parts of Britain and America. Even in the 18th century they enjoyed many un-Quakerly comforts, and in the 19th century several of the Darbys who had developed sophisticated artistic tastes and lived in luxury, moved over to the Church of England.

78 *Mary Bosanquet, depicted before the time of her marriage to the Rev. John Fletcher in 1781.*

Many new Anglican churches were built and many more were restored in the course of the 19th century. The architect who probably contributed most to this process was S. Pountney Smith of Shrewsbury, who was responsible for the churches at Harley, Hope Bowdler, Leaton and Uffington. He frequently used decorative tiles from Jackfield, as in the restoration of Battlefield church, and found new uses for the old masonry which he displaced. The completion of All Saints', Castlefields, in 1876, replacing an earlier temporary building, marked the arrival of the Oxford Movement in Shrewsbury. Two village churches reflected the skills and eccentricities of their Victorian incumbents. At Middleton in Chirbury the Rev. Waldegrave Brewster carved the ends of the benches, the font and the capitals. John Parker, vicar of St Michael, Llanyblodwell, designed an extraordinarily individualist church, with a detached octagonal tower. Several leading national architects worked on Shropshire churches. George Edmund Street restored Upton Magna and Clun parish churches, and designed St John the Evangelist , Lyneal, in 1870 and St John Baptist, Withington in 1874, but St George's, Oakengates must rank as one of the best of his early works. George Gilbert Scott built the church of St Michael Welshampton in 1863. The outstanding late 19th-century church in the county is All Saints', Richards Castle, a large and subtle composition by Richard Norman Shaw, built in 1891.

In 1773 the only public Roman Catholic chapel in the county was in Shrewsbury, although there were seven in private houses. By 1839 there were nine Catholic places of worship, and in 1850, when the Pope restored territorial dioceses in England, Shrewsbury became the seat of a bishop, and a cathedral designed by E.W. Pugin was completed in 1856.

Analyses of the 1851 religious census suggest that the level of church attendance in the south-western corner of the county was exceptionally low by national standards, while that in Shrewsbury was higher than average, and that in the coalfield a little below average. Church attendances varied widely. St Luke's, Ironbridge had an evening congregation of 700 on census Sunday, and Christ Church, Wellington one of 538, but the largest congregation of the day at St Laurence, Ludlow was only 210, a lower total than

79 *A pew end in the church of Holy Trinity, Middleton in Chirbury (SO297994), carved by the Rev. Waldegrave Brewster.*

80 *A capital in the church of Holy Trinity, Middleton in Chirbury (SO297994), carved by the Rev. Waldegrave Brewster.*

81 *The former Primitive Methodist church at Cockshutford (SO58-3850), a squatter settlement under the slopes of Nordy Bank in the parish of Clee St Margaret. The church was built in 1862 for a congregation who had probably been followers of Joanna Southcott at the time of the 1851 Religious Census.*

at the evening services at the local Primitive Methodist and Wesleyan chapels which attracted 300 and 344 people respectively.

The history of religion in Shropshire is enlivened by the presence of several small but remarkable groups. The last of the Non-Juror bishops, the spiritual descendants of those who refused to accept William and Mary as monarchs in place of James II, was William Cartwright, apothecary of Mardol, Shrewsbury, who was consecrated bishop in 1780, held services in his own home, and appeared in the streets in episcopal purple. Bridgnorth was a stronghold of the Holy Catholic Apostolic Church, founded by Edward Irving. The present Castle Hall is a much-altered Irvingite meeting house. The census returns for Bridgnorth reveal the presence in the town of several 'angels', the ministers of the church. The Disciples of Christ, or Campbellites, founded in the United States by Alexander Campbell, a Baptist Scots migrant, established a meeting in Shrewsbury about 1839, and by 1851 there were also congregations at Ellesmere and Tetchill. Alexander Campbell visited Shrewsbury on 9-11 June 1847. A congregation of Millenarians, or followers of Joanna Southcott, were worshipping at Cockshutford, at the foot of Nordy Bank, in 1851.

14

Revolutions in Industry

In the context of national history the most significant events in Shropshire's past were the changes in the second half of the 18th century, when, for a few decades, Shropshire was the leading iron-producing area in Britain and the scene of many innovations, and the Ironbridge Gorge attracted engineers, writers and artists from all over the western world.

Shropshire's industry was based on its mineral resources. There is some evidence of medieval coal working but the first significant industrial development was the growth of coal mining in the parishes of Broseley, Madeley and Benthall in the second half of the 16th century. It has been estimated that the population of Broseley increased ten times between the 1570s and the 1670s. Two important innovations took place in the Severn Gorge in the 17th century. The longwall system of mining was developed, enabling the recovery of a larger proportion of the coal in a seam than had hitherto been possible, and by 1605 two wooden railways had been built in Broseley parish on land belonging to James Clifford. The region prospered

82 *Remains of the Madeley Wood (or Bedlam) blast furnaces (SJ678033) which operated for about 80 years from the mid-1750s. The furnace remains have been partially excavated and restored by the Ironbridge Gorge Museum Trust.*

by sending coal down the river, moving much of it to the riverside wharves by wooden railways. By 1700 much of the output of coal in the Gorge was being employed in manufacturing; for smelting lead ore, for boiling brine to make salt, for the extraction of tar, for firing tobacco pipes and pottery and for the manufacture of glass.

Shropshire's ironworks were important long before the Industrial Revolution of the mid-18th century. Three bloomery furnaces, making wrought-iron in small quantities by direct reduction, were recorded in the Coalbrookdale coalfield in the 1530s. During the 16th century most iron came to be made by the two-stage process. Iron ore was reduced with charcoal and limestone in a blast furnace to cast-iron in the form of 'pigs', rectangular lumps of iron, so called because in the form in which they were cast they appeared to be piglets feeding from a sow. Cast-iron has a carbon content of about four per cent. It is strong in compression and can be cast into intricate shapes, but there were few uses for it in the 17th century. Most pig iron was converted into wrought-iron at a forge, consisting of two hearths, a finery and a chafery, and a hammer which shaped the iron into blooms, which were rolled into rods or plates in a rolling mill. Some was cut into thin rods, suitable for use by craftsmen, in a slitting mill.

83 *A foundry at Coalbrookdale in the 1830s. (From* The Book of Trades *(ed. 1837), Ironbridge Gorge Museum Trust, Elton Collection.)*

The first blast furnace in Shropshire was probably built on Shirlett Common in the 1540s. Another was built by the manor mill at Shifnal in 1564. Between 1600 and 1750 many ironworks were built in Shropshire, forming part of a network which extended from the Lake District to South Wales. All the works used charcoal as their fuel and water as their source of power. Iron was exchanged at various stages of manufacture between the works. Supplies of charcoal were a limiting factor in the growth of ironmaking. Charcoal was made from wood of up to 20 years' growth, which was grown as a crop in coppices. The market for charcoal was dominated by large combines, like those of the Walkers of Bringewood and the Boycott partnership on the Middle Severn.

There were two groups of blast furnaces in Shropshire, one using ore from the Coalbrookdale coalfield and the other drawing it from the coal measures on the Clee Hills. The majority of forges stood in the valleys of the Worfe, the Tern, the Cound Brook and the Rea. Bridgnorth was the focus of the iron trade, receiving iron from the Clee Hills for dispatch to forges in other counties, and pig-iron from the Forest of Dean and America for Shropshire forges. There were also several ironworks in the Oswestry area.

John Weld and many other people in the 17th century had looked forward to the use of mineral fuel in the smelting of iron. A small charcoal-fired blast furnace could operate for ever on the annual crops produced from 2,000 acres of coppiced woodland, but in the early 18th century other uses for land appeared increasingly profitable and, if there was enough charcoal to sustain existing works, there was certainly insufficient land to provide for any expansion in their number. In 1708 the blast furnace at Coalbrookdale, which stood derelict after an explosion, was leased by Abraham Darby, the first of four men to bear that name. A native of the Black Country, Darby had been apprenticed in Birmingham and had worked as an ironfounder in Bristol. He was concerned with the affairs of the Severn Gorge as early as 1706 when he witnessed a deed relating to the Quaker burial ground at Broseley, and probably had interests in a brass works which had been established in the Gorge. Darby rebuilt the blast furnace at the ironworks and when he began to smelt iron in

84 The industrial landscape of East Shropshire. a view of a furnace complex near Wellington painted in 1821 by Francis Nicholson.

85 *The dining room at Rosehill House, Coalbrookdale, built in the 1730s and occupied by several generations of the Darby family. The portrait shows Abraham Darby IV. Rosehill House was re-stored by the Ironbridge Gorge Museum Trust in the 1980s as an ironmaster's dwelling of the mid-19th century (SJ666050).*

January 1708-09 he used coke made from local coal and not charcoal as his fuel. The iron produced was suitable for making castings, which was Darby's principal interest, but it did not forge into good wrought-iron. Darby and his partners developed a forge, the Tern works, at Atcham, near to the site now occupied by the mansion at Attingham. At Tern were mills for rolling and slitting both brass and iron. Its output of finished iron was one of the largest of any forge in England. Darby was also concerned with a copper smelter in Coalbrookdale, for which he sought ores in 1710 from mines at Harmer Hill north of Shrewsbury. Before his death in 1717 Darby had built a second blast furnace in Coalbrookdale. By the early 1720s his successors were producing cast-iron cylinders for Newcomen steam engines and selling pots and pans throughout the Borderland. The brassworks in Coalbrookdale seems to have ceased operation in 1714, when its equipment was carried downstream to Bristol. The copper smelter probably worked until the time of Darby's death.

The second Abraham Darby entered the Coalbrookdale Works at the age of 17 in 1728. In the early 1740s he began to employ a steam engine to return the water which had flowed over the water wheels operating the bellows of the blast furnaces back to the pool above the Upper Furnace, thus setting up a circulation system which made the ironworks independent of rainfall. In the early 1750s he discovered that iron of good quality for forging could be made using coke as his fuel. In 1754 he and his partner, Thomas Goldney, began to construct a new blast furnace at Horsehay about two miles north of Coalbrookdale. They had difficulty in making the furnace pool watertight but, once put into blast in May 1755, the furnace proved successful. The following year saw the outbreak of the Seven Years War, and within four years nine furnaces were built in the district. The Shropshire coalfield became the leading iron-producing area in Great Britain.

86 *A wooden pit headstock at the Blists Hill Open Air Museum.*

Innovations in the district were numerous; the first iron railway wheels and track, the Iron Bridge, John Wilkinson's iron boat, *The Trial*, launched in 1787, and the steam railway locomotive built by Richard Trevithick at Coalbrookdale in 1802. In 1784 Lord Dundonald began to make coke in closed ovens, condensing the gases given off to produce tar and varnishes. About 1800 William Reynolds the ironmaster was experimenting with some of these oils to drive an engine. Dundonald and Reynolds planned an alkali works at Coalport, where by using coal, limestone and common salt to make soda they proposed to manufacture glass, fertilisers, dyestuffs and soap. Reynolds had interests in another alkali works at Wombridge and a glassworks at Wrockwardine Wood. The first porcelain manufactory in Shropshire was set up about 1772 by Thomas Turner at Caughley. Turner's former apprentices, the brothers John and Thomas Rose, provided the expertise for two factories established in William Reynolds' new town of Coalport in the 1790s. The coalfield became the centre of attention for people from many parts of the world, who, whether their primary interest was in engineering, social change or spectacular scenery, journeyed to Shropshire to walk across the Iron Bridge, to watch iron tapped from the Coalbrookdale furnaces, to ride on the carriages of the Hay inclined plane, to buy china from John Rose at Coalport and to suffer the excruciating aural pains inflicted by Alexander Brodie's cannon boring mill at the Calcutts.

Workers were attracted to the Coalbrookdale coalfield from other parts of Shropshire and from Wales. They found high wages, which were won at the price of long hours, and, in the mines, of hazardous working conditions. Until the 1840s it was customary for blast furnacemen to work seven 12-hour shifts a week. In the mines there were several fatal accidents a month, some caused by roof falls and a few by gas explosions, but more by avoidable falls into shafts. Women were employed on pit banks separating nodules of iron ore from the clays or shales in which they had been brought to the surface. They gained competence in carrying heavy loads on their heads and used this skill each summer when they migrated to London to pick strawberries and carry them to Covent Garden. Traditionally the girls remained in the Metropolis for other harvests through August, and returned home for Oakengates Wake at the end of September.

87 *A foot rid or adit at the Blists Hill Open Air Museum.*

88   The Hoffman kiln at the Lilleshall Company's brickworks at Donnington Wood (SJ712114), Telford, one of a series of photographs taken for the company in the 1930s.

The pre-eminence of the Coalbrookdale coalfield was not maintained in the 19th century. In 1805 the area was producing about 50,000 tons of iron a year, about a fifth of the national output. By 1869, the year of peak production in Shropshire, the output was all but 200,000 tons, a mere two per cent of national output. Nevertheless several companies in the coalfield were celebrated for the excellence of their products. From about 1838 the Coalbrookdale Works began to make art castings in iron, for which it gained an international reputation after mounting a successful display at the Great Exhibition in 1851. In 1861 the Lilleshall Company constructed an engineering works in the settlement known as Pain's Lane which lined the course of Watling Street on the borders of the townships of Priorslee and Wrockwardine Wood, and its stationary engines, pumps and locomotives were sold in many countries. A public meeting on 19 December 1859 had resolved that the community would henceforth be known as St George's. In Jackfield in the Severn Gorge the decorative tile factories built by Messrs. Craven Dunnill in 1874 and by Maw & Co. in 1884 made ceramic products for public buildings in all parts of the world in the closing decades of the century. From the 1870s the iron industry declined, and by 1885 production was back to the levels of the early 1800s. The population of the mining parishes fell rapidly. There were 9,200 people in Dawley in 1881, but only 6,996 a decade later.

In the late 17th and early 18th centuries the coal mining communities on the slopes of Titterstone Clee grew substantially. Coal was sent to local towns, iron ore was produced for nearby blast furnaces and coal was employed in the making of tobacco pipes, bricks, tiles, pottery called Clee Hill ware, and, possibly, for glass-making. Most of the miners occupied squatter cottages, of which there were 49 on the wastes of Snitton township alone in 1745, a total which had grown to 68 in 1778. In the late 18th century two coke-fired ironworks were built on Clee Hill. The Cornbrook Furnace was constructed by 1794, although it was only making 292 tons of iron a year in 1805, and was out of blast by the 1820s. The Knowbury works was built in 1804-05. When it was offered for sale in 1851 it included a forge, a rolling mill and a slitting mill, as well as a blast furnace. The mining of coal on the Clee Hills continued into the 20th century, but declined in importance as the quarrying of the local dhustone for road metal expanded.

The building of the Ellesmere Canal and the growing demand from farmers and builders for lime stimulated the sinking of coal pits in the St Martin's and Weston Rhyn areas. Much of the growth in the coalfield in the 19th century was in the parish of St Martin's, where the number of miners grew from 97 in 1851 to 299 in 1881. In the Wyre Forest coalfield a blast furnace at Billingsley using coal and ore from local mines operated between 1801 and 1812. Investment in the Oswestry and Wyre Forest coalfields continued into the 20th century. By 1928 the colliery at Ifton in St Martin's parish employed some 1,357 men, making it the largest ever to

89 *Ifton Colliery at St Martin's (SJ32-2374), shortly before its closure in 1968. 1,357 men worked there in 1828, the largest number ever to be employed at a Shropshire colliery.*

90 Wrought-iron kibbles at the Snailbeach mine (SJ378023) which were used for raising lead ore to the surface. When this picture was taken in 1967 the kibbles were still full of ore.

operate in Shropshire. It closed in 1968. The mining company at Highley was formed in 1870. In the 1930s the colliery incorporated new workings on the opposite bank of the Severn, and employed 1,250 men in the 1950s. It closed in 1967. In the Shrewsbury coalfield, whose generally small collieries were scattered between Haughmond Hill and the Breiddens, most coal was supplied to limekilns and to rural brickworks in addition to meeting local demands for domestic fuel, although at Pontesford coal was used for smelting lead ores. The last pit in the coalfield, at Hanwood, closed in 1942.

The lead mines of South Shropshire were for a time some of the most productive in Britain. Large-scale developments began in the second half of the 18th century. Boulton & Watt steam engines were installed at the Bog mine in 1777 and 1789 and at the Old Grit in 1783. The rich Snailbeach mine was leased in 1782 by Thomas Lovett of Chirk, who proceeded to develop a coalmine at Pontesbury and an adjacent smelthouse. More lead mines were sunk in the 19th century and the area reached its zenith in the 1870s when ten mines were producing more than 7,000 tons of lead ore a year, about ten per cent of the national output. The 1880s saw the beginning of a sharp decline. The Snailbeach Mine, after several temporary closures, finally ceased work in 1911, bringing the production of lead in Shropshire to an end, although several mines continued to produce barytes.

Several carpet mills, offshoots of the old established Kidderminster trade, were built in Bridgnorth from the late 1790s, and a mill for spinning hemp and flax built at Eardington in 1794 may have been associated with this development. The weavers in mid-Wales concentrated increasingly on flannel in the late 18th century, which led ultimately to the disappearance of the traditional Shrewsbury market for Welsh cloth in 1797. There were several offshoots of the new trade in Shropshire. In 1800 the stock of Thomas Child, flannel manufacturer of Barker Street, Shrewsbury was sold up. It consisted of carding machinery and several looms, with a chestnut mare to work the wheel. At the Isle, upstream from Shrewsbury at the neck of the great meander on the Severn, a tunnel was cut to power a flannel manufactory which by 1824 included two carding engines, jennies, looms, and two fulling mills.

Shropshire also had links with the Midlands cotton industry. In 1790 a woollen factory was built in Shrewsbury at the junction of Longden Coleham and Coleham Head. It failed in 1795 when it consisted of two five-storey buildings and one of four storeys. In 1803 it was acquired by

91 Above left. *The world's first iron-framed building, the former flax mill at Ditherington, Shrewsbury (SJ499138) built to the design of Charles Bage in 1796-97. The mill was used for the manufacture of linen thread and yarn by John Marshall & Co. until 1886. About ten years later it was converted to a maltings by William Jones & Co, and served that purpose until 1987, except during the Second World War when it was a barracks.*

92 Above right. *The fourth floor of the Shropshire Maltings, Ditherington, Shrewsbury (SJ499138), formerly the Ditherington Flax Mill. The cast-iron cross beams are supported by the external walls and the three lines of columns. Brick arches spring from the beams and carry the floor above. There are spaces at the tops of the columns in the central line through which passes line shafting which powered machines for spinning flax. On the floor are piles of barley just removed from the wetting vat. The barley was left out for several days until it started to sprout, after which it was taken to the kiln at the end of the buildings.*

93 Right. *The south elevation of the late 18th-century pumping engine house of a colliery at Pontesford (SJ410065), the most imposing industrial monument of the Shrewsbury coalfield.*

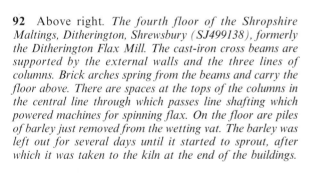

94 *The China Works at Coalport.*

a Mancunian, Charles Hulbert, who used it for weaving cotton, in association with a spinning mill at Llangollen and a calico printing works on the Morda near Oswestry. Hulbert soon found it was more profitable to sell fabrics made elsewhere. From 1809 parts of the mill were let to other manufacturers and some portions were used for workers' housing. An attempt to introduce 30 steam looms was resisted by the workers in 1812, and two years later Hulbert moved out to work as an auctioneer, printer, stationer, bookseller and writer. He sold the site in 1825. Another cotton mill was working in Broseley in 1792, although little is known of it. A further mill was built on the River Rea in Stottesdon parish about 1794, probably on the site of the former Prescot Forge. It was offered for sale under a commission of bankruptcy in 1804, and was probably never again used for its original purpose.

The manufacture of linen on a domestic scale was widespread in Shropshire in the 18th century but subsequent large-scale production owed little to these humble origins. In 1788 John Marshall, a Leeds linen merchant, built a flax spinning mill using an existing patent process. When his partners left him in 1793 he looked for other sources of capital and was joined by Benjamin and Thomas Benyon from Shrewsbury, who invested £9,000 in the concern. After a fire in a newly-built mill in Leeds on 13 February 1796, the Benyons insisted on constructing a replacement on the banks of the Shrewsbury Canal in the county town. A revolutionary fireproof building was designed by Charles Bage, a Shrewsbury wine merchant and surveyor. He was a friend of Thomas Telford and William Reynolds, and the correspondent of William Strutt of Belper who had pioneered the use of upright columns in mills in Derbyshire. The flax mill had brick walls and an internal iron frame of cruciform section uprights, and beams supporting brick arches which formed the floors of the storeys above. In 1804 the partnership of the Benyons and Bage with John Marshall came to an end. The latter retained the Ditherington mill, while the former partners built a new mill in Castlefields. After the deaths of the Benyons the Castlefields mill was demolished early in 1837, but an iron-framed outbuilding survived and was used for linen weaving before its conversion into dwellings in the 1850s. Bage had left the Benyons in 1816 to set up his own flax-weaving business in a brick-vaulted mill in the Shrewsbury suburb of Kingsland, but he died in 1822 and his widow sold the building to Thomas Burr in 1829 for use as a lead factory. Marshall's mill provided employment for several hundred people until 1886 when the Marshalls decided to close down the whole of their flax-manufacturing operation. The building was converted to a maltings around 1900, and served that purpose until 1987.

95 *The ruins of an engine house at the Snailbeach lead mine.*

For a short period in the late 18th century Shropshire was one of the world's pioneering industrial regions. Since that time one part of the county after another has suffered the pains of de-industrialisation. Iron smelting, lead mining, the production of coal from deep mines, the manufacture of linen and woollen cloth, have all ceased in Shropshire, a consequence of that very change in the nature of economic activity of which the county's industrial revolution was part.

IX *The* Feathers Hotel, *Ludlow (S0513746), dating from c.1611, the supreme achievement of the school of carpenters who worked in the town in the late 16th and early 17th centuries.*

X *High Victorian architecture in Shrewsbury—The Eye, Ear and Throat Hospital, designed by C.O. Ellison of Liverpool, incorporating much ornamental terracotta from the works of J.C. Edwards at Ruabon, and opened in 1881 (SJ498122).*

XI *The restored GWR 4-6-0 locomotive No. 6000* King George V *moves an enthusiasts' special train along the Shrewsbury & Hereford Railway out of Shrewsbury (SJ496112) on 3 October 1981.*

XII *The canal junction at Welsh Frankton (SJ370319). The line to the right links the routes to Shrewsbury and to the Montgomeryshire Canal with the main line.*

15

Changing Patterns of Transport

In 1750 Shropshire was crossed by few main roads and had no stage coach services. Its internal roads were of poor repute. Archdeacon Plymley wrote about 1800 that the roads around Clee St Margaret were 'narrow and deep and during winter impossible to all except the natives who are well acquainted with their miry depths'.

96 *A turnpike trust tollhouse at Minsterley.*

Shropshire's principal link with the outside world in the 18th century was the River Severn. Barges carried away wool, lead ore, cheese and leather, and brought from Bristol the cloth, tobacco, spirits, spices and groceries sold in the county's market towns. They conveyed to customers the coal dug in the Severn Gorge, and acted as a production line for the charcoal iron industry. Bridgnorth was an entrepôt for much of the north-west Midlands. Throughout the second half of the 18th century passenger wherries operated time-tabled services from Shrewsbury to Worcester and Gloucester.

Barges sailed when the water was sufficiently deep and ceased operations when it was not. In periods of low rainfall they might remain at their moorings for nine months in a year. The barges used their sails, but their progress downstream depended largely on the current, and in the upstream direction they were pulled by gangs of men known as bow-haulers, until the construction of towpaths at the end of the 18th century made possible haulage by horses. Most vessels in Shropshire were small barges of up to 30 tons which carried coal. Larger vessels, up to 80 tons, called trows (although that term sometimes indicated any vessel on the river) were able to sail on the lower Severn below Gloucester and up the Avon to Bristol. Much Shropshire traffic was transhipped from small to large vessels at Bewdley or Gloucester. Attempts to improve the navigation by building locks were resisted by the bargemen. A scheme devised by William Jessop was put forward in 1784-86, and was rejected by the House of Commons after many protests. When the Severn was improved in the 1840s the locks did not extend upstream from Stourport.

97 *A crude stone milepost on the old Bishop's Castle turnpike road across Cothercot Hill to Shrewsbury.*

The Severn Navigation declined during the 19th century. The Montgomeryshire Canal took away traffic from the upper reaches, and the linking of the Shrewsbury Canal with the national waterways network in 1835 reduced loadings from the county town. The 1841 census reveals 17 watermen in Shrewsbury but there were only two a decade later. Traffic below Coalbrookdale was reduced by the opening of the Severn Valley

97

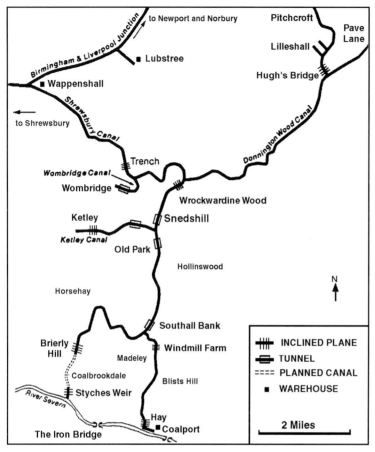

98 *Tub-boat canals in the Coalbrookdale Coalfield.*

Railway in 1862, but some bricks and iron castings were still being carried in the 1880s. Commercial navigation ended on Friday 25 January 1895 when a barge laden with firebricks hit one of the piers of Bridgnorth Bridge and sank 260 yards further downstream.

The principal barge-owning communities in Shropshire were in Shrewsbury, the Severn Gorge and Bridgnorth. The Ship Money returns of the 1630s reveal that there were seven trowmen in the county town. In 1756 ten owners operated 19 vessels, and in 1837 six were working 20 boats. The communities in the Gorge and in Bridgnorth were much larger. In 1756 there were 84 owners of boats in Broseley, Benthall and Madeley working 139 vessels, while in Bridgnorth there were 47 owners with 75 boats. Some of the Bridgnorth owners were rich men who traded with Bristol, like Thomas Andrews who died in 1723 with possessions worth nearly £170. He worked the frigate *Cunney* worth £18, the barge *Hannah* worth £20 and a trow, the *Loving Brother*, worth £80. He kept a public house with 154 gallons of ale in the cellar, vast quantities of linen, a shuffle board and a display of flint glasses and toys. Most barge owners struggled to make a living with one small vessel taking coal on credit from wharves in the Gorge and selling it downstream.

The Statutes of Roads in 1555 and 1562 made roads the responsibility of parishes supervised in each county by Quarter Sessions. Each householder had to work on the roads himself, or provide 'one sufficient labourer in his stead' on six days a year. Work was supervised by parish surveyors, not professionals but usually parishioners who held the office in rotation with such other positions as parish constable or overseer. This obligation to perform 'statute labour' remained until 1839, although after 1662 it was used less and less.

The Tudor system of road administration put the responsibility for upkeep upon those who happened to live alongside the roads concerned. In the depths of the Corvedale or in the hills west of Oswestry this was an equitable system, since few but natives used the roads. In Newport on the great road from London to Chester it meant that parishioners had to pay substantial sums for the benefit of strangers. The system of turnpike trusts, which originated in 1663, was a means of transferring the costs from those who lived near main roads to those who used them. Turnpike trusts established by Acts of Parliament had powers to collect tolls, to acquire land for road improvements, to farm out the collection of tolls to contractors, and to borrow money for improvements. Such trusts transformed the road system in Shropshire.

In the first half of the 18th century most of the routes from London to the main provincial towns were the subject of turnpike legislation. The first Shropshire road to be so treated was that from Shrewsbury to Crackley Bank and Shifnal, offering a choice of routes to London, which was turnpiked in 1726.

The roads turnpiked in the 1750s were mostly networks radiating from market towns. In 1752 the roads from Shrewsbury to Wrexham and Bridgnorth along with the routes southwards from Ludlow towards Worcester and Hereford were turnpiked. In 1756 five turnpike trusts were established in Shropshire as a result of a campaign co-ordinated by John Ashby. In 1771 and 1772 the routes from Wem to Bron-y-Garth and from Burlton to Llanymynech were turnpiked, giving access to lime and limestone from the kilns and quarries on the county's western boundary.

After 1800 many entirely new stretches of road were constructed. South of Ludlow the roads leading to Tenbury and Leominster were re-routed in the 1830s and the old routes stopped up. A new road from Coalbrookdale to Wellington was completed in 1818. In 1833 an Act was obtained for a new road from Minsterley to Churchstoke, through the spectacular scenery of the Hope Valley. In 1843 a road from Morville to Shipton formed a route from Bridgnorth to Ludlow which avoided the necessity to cross the Clee Hills. As railway competition grew the turnpike trustees relinquished their responsibilities, and the last toll-gates in Shropshire were removed in 1893.

99 *A cast-iron milepost on the road from Morville to Shipton, the last new main road to be built in Shropshire in the 19th century, completed in 1843.*

100 *A turnpike tollhouse at Richards Castle (SO509725) at the junction of the new roads south of Ludford Bridge from Ludlow to Worcester and Leominster, laid out in the early 1830s.*

101 *A cast-iron mile-post near the Hundred House, Stockton, on the road from Shifnal to Bridgnorth which was an outlying section of a Staffordshire turnpike trust.*

Many turnpike tollhouses remain throughout Shropshire. Some are single-storey cottages with bow windows and are easily recognisable, but many were of two storeys, not significantly different from others of the period. Many of the surviving mileposts in Shropshire are of cast-iron, triangular in plan, with chamfered triangular tops.

In 1750 passengers from Shrewsbury to London either travelled to Ivetsey Bank to pick up a coach from Chester, or went by Severn wherry to Worcester and thence by road. The first stage coach service from Shrewsbury to London began in 1753, taking 3½ days for the journey, probably including overnight stops. By 1772 it was possible to travel to the capital in 1½ days. About 1774 Robert Lawrence of the *Raven and Bell* began to operate coaches to London. In 1779 he began a thrice weekly service to Holyhead through Ellesmere, and the following year added a second coach through Oswestry, thus being able to offer services on six days a week. In 1781 he moved to the *Lion*, the great inn built a few years previously by John Ashby. Passengers from London to Dublin had previously gone to Holyhead through Chester, but Lawrence succeeded in creating a new route through Shrewsbury. In 1808 the Royal Mail carrying letters for Ireland began to call at the *Lion*. From the 1780s services from Shrewsbury to Bath and Bristol connected with the Holyhead coaches and in the 1790s coaches began to run to Liverpool and Manchester. From the late 1790s Shrewsbury became the terminus of coaches to the Welsh coast which did much to establish Aberystwyth and Barmouth as resorts.

Apart from the *Lion* and the adjacent *Raven and Bell*, the chief coaching inns in Shrewsbury were the *Britannia*, rebuilt in the 1820s on land belonging to the Earl of Tankerville, which had stabling for 150 horses, and the

102 *The* Angel Inn, *Ludlow (SO512745), in the early 19th century when it was the town's principal calling point for stage coaches.*

103 *The* Talbot Hotel, *Shrewsbury (SJ49-1125) designed by Samuel Scoltock and constructed in 1775. Following the opening of main-line railways to Shrewsbury, the hotel was closed in the 1850s and converted to offices. Extensive re-building took place after a fire in the 1980s, although the relief talbot shown in this engraving remains over one of the doorways. The drawing exaggerates the width of Market Street and Swan Hill, the streets bounding the hotel.*

Talbot, designed by Samuel Scoltock and built in 1775 on land belonging to the Ottleys of Pitchford. Coaching in Shrewsbury reached its zenith in the mid-1830s when it was possible to travel to London in 18 hours. The coaches from the *Lion* customarily paraded through the town on the official birthdays of William IV. In 1836 one six-horse and 15 four-horse coaches took part, and were the first vehicles to pass over the new portion of road by the Abbey.

Main line railways brought an end to the prosperity of coaching. The Grand Junction Railway linking Birmingham with Liverpool and Manchester opened in 1837, and the London & Birmingham Railway the following year. Coaches from Shrewsbury to London began to connect with trains at Birmingham, while the northern coaches ran to the station at Whitmore south of Crewe. Through the 1840s the coaches served more and more as feeders to the railways until 1848-49 when Shropshire's own railways were opened. It was not until the 1860s that a through line to the mid-Wales coast was completed, and during the 1850s coach traffic to Aberystwyth and Barmouth prospered, with services bearing such names as the *Exhibition*, which ran in 1851, and the *Nugget* which commemorated the Welsh gold rush of 1854.

During the 25 years after 1815 the route through Shropshire to Holyhead was improved under the direction of Thomas Telford until it was the best road in Europe. In 1810 Telford was asked by a parliamentary committee to survey routes between London and Dublin. He argued that the route through Shrewsbury was the most worthy of improvement, and when the Holyhead Road Commission was established in 1815 he became its surveyor. At first the Commission worked through the turnpike trusts but impatience with their inefficiency led to the setting up of a new Parliamentary Turnpike Commission in 1819, which took over complete responsibility for the roads

104 *A plateway wag-gon preserved at the Museum of Iron, Coalbrookdale.*

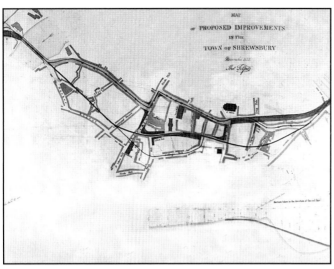

105 Left. *Thomas Telford's proposals for improving the line of the Holyhead Road between the English Bridge and the Welsh Bridge in Shrewsbury, 1823.*

106 Below. *The tollhouse built to the design of Thomas Telford at Shelton (SJ466133), just west of Shrewsbury on the Holyhead Road, and rebuilt at the Blists Hill Open Air Museum (SJ694033), Ironbridge, in 1972-73.*

107 Bottom. *The Holyhead Road in Shropshire.*

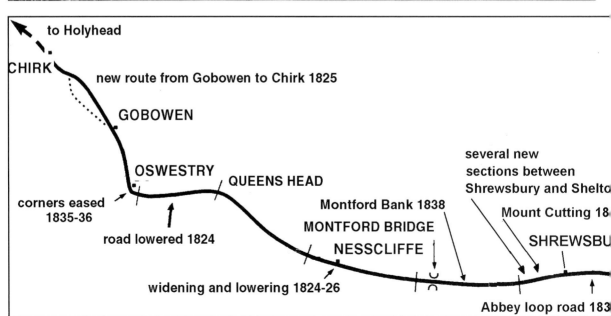

west of Shrewsbury. Some large-scale improvements in Shropshire were delayed by Telford's hope that he might build a direct route from Wellington to Chirk avoiding Shrewsbury. In Shrewsbury he proposed dramatic improvements which would have involved much demolition but these plans were never realised. A new road avoiding the congestion in Shifnal market place was built between 1828 and 1830. A road around Overley Hill, 'the greatest obstacle in the way of travelling', was opened in December 1835. A new route over Montford Bank between Shrewsbury and Montford Bridge was completed in July 1838. Mileposts of a standard type were installed all the way from Shrewsbury to Holyhead in 1828, and two tollhouses of the standard pattern used on the mainland were built in Shropshire, one at Oswestry, which remains *in situ*, and one at Shelton, which was removed to the Blists Hill Open Air Museum in 1972.

108 *The masonry aqueduct by which Josiah Clowes carried the Shrewsbury Canal over the River Roden at Roddington.*

The same parliamentary report which noted the completion of the improvements at Montford Bank and Overley Hill in 1838 mentioned the opening of the railways linking London with Lancashire. Long distance traffic fell off and the opening of the Shrewsbury-Wolverhampton railway in 1849 was

> the cause of removing nearly all the traffic from the Turnpike trusts as if by magic ... and the road that was considered the best in England, namely London to Holyhead, in a few months time was almost deserted.

In 1851 the commissioners concluded that they could no longer justify spending public money on its maintenance.

Shropshire was served by four canal systems. The canal authorised in 1791 to link Leominster with the Severn was never completed but ran only from the collieries near Southnet in Worcestershire to Leominster. Three sections passed through the southernmost extremities of Shropshire, and a wharf at Woofferton supplied Ludlow with coal. The canal was never profitable and closed in 1858, some of its bed being used for the railway from Bewdley to Woofferton.

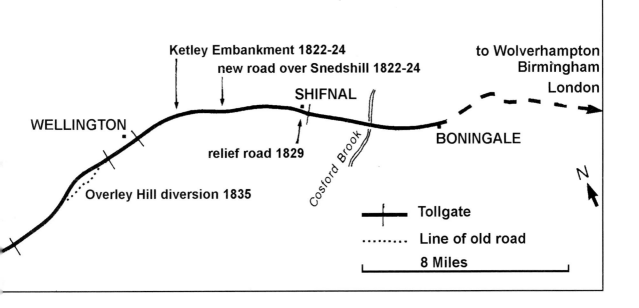

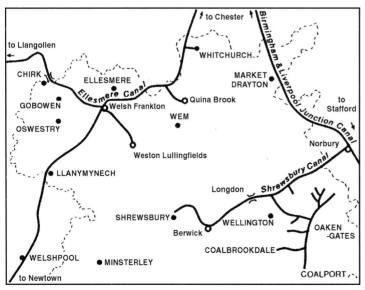

109 Top. *Beech House, Ellesmere (SJ400342), the one-time headquarters of the Ellesmere Canal Company, at the junction of the Llangollen line of the canal with the branch which leads into the centre of the town. The central room on the first floor was the boardroom.*

110 Middle. *The iron aqueduct across the River Tern at Longdon (SJ617156) on the Shrewsbury Canal, built to the design of Thomas Telford in 1795-96, utilising the stone abutments of an aqueduct started by Josiah Clowes, but destroyed by a flood in February 1795.*

111 Left. *Canals in Shropshire.*

The earliest canal system in Shropshire was the network in the Coalbrookdale Coalfield, on which tub boats, simple rectangular vessels measuring 20ft. x 6ft. 4in. (6m. x 1.9m.), were employed. The Donnington Wood Canal, a private venture by Earl Gower and Co., was built in the 1760s. It ran from mines at Donnington Wood to Pave Lane on the Newport-Wolverhampton road, with a branch to the limestone quarries at Lilleshall.

112 *A wrought-iron tub boat of 19th-century date in the Blists Hill Open Air Museum.*

In the 1780s two further short private canals were built by the ironmaster William Reynolds at Wombridge and Ketley. They, and the Donnington Wood Canal, were linked by the Shropshire Canal, authorised in 1788, which ran across the coalfield to the Severn at a terminus which received the name Coalport, and to a wharf at Brierly Hill above Coalbrookdale. Inclined planes, using some of the principles of one built on the Ketley Canal, were used to achieve changes of level at Wrockwardine Wood, Windmill Farm and the Hay. In 1793 an Act of Parliament authorised the extension of the tub-boat system to Shrewsbury. The new line joined the Wombridge Canal at Trench, where there was an inclined plane. It descended through 11 guillotine locks to Eyton, crossed the Tern and Roden on aqueducts, and passed through the 970-yard Berwick tunnel to enter Shrewsbury from the north. The aqueduct over the Tern at Longdon was begun by the engineer Josiah Clowes but he died, and the preliminary works were destroyed in a flood. Thomas Telford became the company's engineer, and under his direction an iron aqueduct was cast by William Reynolds & Co. at Ketley. The first stage of the canal from Trench to Long Lane was opened in December 1794, but it was not until February 1797 that it was completed to Shrewsbury.

The Ellesmere Canal Company founded in 1793 hoped to create a trunk waterway linking the Mersey, the Dee and the Severn, but its attempt to reach Shrewsbury ended in a field near Weston Lullingfields. After heroically crossing the valleys of the Dee and the Ceiriog by aqueducts at Chirk and Pontcysyllte, its projected line across the Wrexham coalfield to Chester was abandoned in favour of a route across the North Shropshire mosses to Hurlstone where a junction was made with the older Chester Canal in 1805. A branch from Welsh Frankton joined this line with the Montgomeryshire Canal at Carreghofa near the county boundary. The construction of the canal was overseen by Thomas Telford from Shrewsbury Castle. The Ellesmere Canal gained a modestly prosperous living by serving the mine owners, quarrymen, millers and farmers of Shropshire and North Wales.

113 *A winding drum on an inclined plane at Pant, part of a primitive railway by which limestone was conveyed from Llanymynech Hill to the banks of the Ellesmere Canal.*

The fourth Shropshire canal system was the Birmingham & Liverpool Junction Canal, authorised in 1826 to link the West Midlands with Merseyside. Its 40-mile main line from Autherley near Wolverhampton to the Ellesmere & Chester Canal at Nantwich enters Shropshire 1½ miles south-east of Cheswardine. A branch from Norbury through Newport to Wappenshall linked the Shrewsbury Canal to the national network. Wappenshall became a busy transhipment point, dispatching coal, iron and bricks, and receiving shop goods for the whole of the coalfield. In 1844 it was supplemented by a second transhipment wharf at Lubstree. The junction at Wappenshall was located between the ninth and tenth of the locks on the

114   A narrow boat passing through the lock at Newport (SJ744195) on the Wappenshall branch of the Birmingham & Liverpool Junction Canal, c.1910. The tall building on the right now forms part of the sawmill at the Blists Hill Open Air Museum at Ironbridge.

flight descending from Trench. The tenth and eleventh locks were widened, enabling standard narrow boats, 7ft. (2.1m) in beam, to reach Shrewsbury, but only specially-built narrow boats, 70ft. (21m) long but only 6ft. 4in. (1.9m) wide and called 'Shroppies', could reach the basin at Trench. The linking of Shrewsbury to the national canal system stimulated the construction of the Butter Market in Howard Street, while three national carrying companies built canalside warehouses off the Castle Foregate.

In 1846 the Shropshire Union Canal Company incorporated the Birmingham & Liverpool Junction, the Ellesmere & Chester, Shropshire, Shrewsbury and Montgomeryshire companies, and was afterwards taken over by the London & North Western Railway. The tub-boat system was in a ramshackle condition and most of the main line of the Shropshire Canal was used for the railway from Hadley to Coalport which opened in 1861.

Shropshire was one of the birthplaces of the English railway. The first recorded line in the county ran from the Birch Leasows near Broseley church to the Calcutts on the banks of the Severn, a distance of about one mile, and was operating in 1605. Several other lines were built during the 17th century linking mines in Broseley and Madeley to the River Severn. In 1729 iron railway wheels were cast at Coalbrookdale, and probably for vehicles on Richard Hartshorne's new railway from Little Wenlock to a wharf at Strethill. In 1767 iron rails were cast by the Coalbrookdale Company. They were the upper portions for two-level rails which had been in use for some time previously. About 1790 flanged L-section plate rails, the invention of John Curr of Sheffield, were introduced. Plateways continued to be built in the coalfield in the 19th century, and one at Horsehay, which was used in 1943-44 to convey parts for barges used in the Normandy landings, remained in operation until 1970. During the 18th century most of the important innovations in railway technology were made in Shropshire, a sequence which reached its culmination when Richard Trevithick built a steam railway locomotive at Coalbrookdale in 1802. Shropshire only acquired its first main-line railway in 1848, some 18 years after the first of its kind, the Liverpool & Manchester Railway, commenced operation.

The Shrewsbury & Chester Railway opened late in 1848. The following year the joint Shrewsbury & Birmingham and Shropshire Union line from Shrewsbury to Wellington was opened, the former extending to Wolverhampton and the latter to Stafford. A period of intense railway politicking followed, with the LNWR attempting to bully the two Shrewsbury-based companies into a merger. Instead they came to an agreement with the

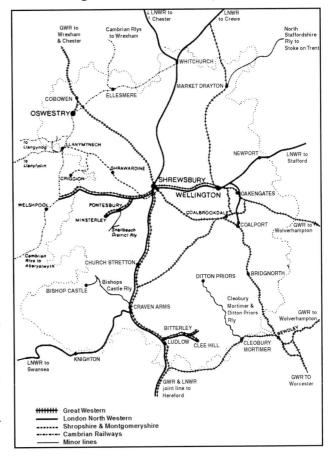

115 *Shropshire's Railways.*

Great Western Railway, and formed a junction with that company at Wolverhampton in 1854, merging with it the following year, and creating a through route from Paddington to Merseyside. The line from Shrewsbury to Hereford was opened to Ludlow in 1852 and completed in 1853. It was constructed cheaply by the contracting firm of Brassey & Field, with severe gradients and sharp curves. It prospered as a route between the North of England and South Wales, particularly after the LNWR opened its line from Shrewsbury to Crewe in 1858. In 1862 it came jointly under the control of the LNWR and the GWR and, after the opening of the Severn Tunnel in 1886, it flourished as a long-distance passenger route.

At Wellington and Shrewsbury and throughout the lengths of the Shrewsbury & Hereford and Shrewsbury & Welshpool lines the locomotives, rolling stock and staff of both the LNWR and the GWR could be seen. The companies competed fiercely for traffic to Birmingham and London, but the opening of the GWR line from Paddington to Banbury through Bicester in 1910 shortened its route and it gained most of the traffic.

116 *A local passenger train at Newport (SJ751183) on the LNWR line from Wellington to Stafford, c.1910.*

117 *The autotrain for Gobowen prepares to leave Oswestry (SJ295298) in May 1963, headed by Great Western 0-4-2T locomotive 1432. In the background are wagons loaded with ballast from the quarries at Llynclys.*

In the north of the county the headquarters of the Cambrian Railways were at Oswestry. The company also served Llanymynech, Ellesmere and Whitchurch, but its main function was to provide a link to the resorts of the mid-Wales coast. The North Staffordshire Railway penetrated into Shropshire with the last few miles of its branch from Silverdale to Market Drayton which opened in 1870.

The Snailbeach District Railways which opened in 1877, formed a narrow-gauge system linking Pontesbury on the Minsterley branch with the lead mines on the Stiperstones. In 1923, after its traffic in lead ore had ceased, it was acquired by the celebrated Colonel Stephens and became remarkable for its eccentricities. The Bishop's Castle Railway, opened in 1865, ran from the Shrewsbury & Hereford line near Craven Arms to Lydham Heath where trains reversed to run into Bishop's Castle. It was renowned neither for speed, efficiency nor punctuality, and operated for a time in defiance of creditors' bailiffs. In the extreme north west the Glyn Valley Tramway linking the slate quarries of Glyn Ceiriog with the out-side world had its eastern terminus in Shropshire on the banks of the Ellesmere Canal at Gledrid when it opened in 1874. The company abandoned the Shropshire portion of its system in 1888 when it changed from horse to steam traction, and built a new route into Chirk. The most eccentric of Shropshire railways was the Potteries, Shrewsbury & North Wales, which was intended to run to Porth Dinllaen. It was opened in 1866 from Shrewsbury's second station by the Abbey, to Llanymynech and Criggion, through some of the most sparsely populated parts of the county. The line was closed for three decades from 1880, had an unconventional existence as the Shropshire & Montgomeryshire Light Railway under Colonel Stephens in the 1920s and '30s, and was remarkably revived by the War Department to serve ammunition depots in the Nesscliff area between 1941 and 1960.

118 An LNWR 0-8-0 locomotive of a type which worked on most of the company's lines in Shropshire.

During the 1850s and '60s the railways spread to serve almost every settlement of consequence in the county; Ruyton-XI-Towns and Clun, each with a population of around a thousand in 1901, were the largest places which lacked stations. In the years before the First World War Shrewsbury was one of the principal railway junctions in Britain. Great Western trains from Birkenhead (Woodside) to London (Paddington) passed through and from 1895 some conveyed through coaches to and from Aberystwyth, Barmouth and Pwllheli. Trains from Birkenhead travelled through to Bournemouth on the London & South Western Railway, Brighton and Eastbourne on the London, Brighton & South Coast, and Dover and Ramsgate on the South Eastern. London and North Western trains left for Euston via Stafford, some with through coaches from Aberystwyth, and from Swansea (Victoria) which had come via the Central Wales line and Craven Arms. From 1889 long distance services over the Hereford line linked Manchester, Liverpool, Glasgow and Edinburgh with Kingswear, Plymouth, Penzance and Cardiff. Every night travelling post offices were to be seen in the station. During the previous 150 years Shropshire's isolation had effectively been brought to an end.

119 The signalbox on the Shrewsbury & Hereford Railway at Bromfield. This was the standard design used on the line and several other examples survive in Shropshire.

16

Victorian Market Towns

The market town in the 19th century was, like Thomas Hardy's Casterbridge, 'the pole, focus or nerve-knot of the surrounding country life', the venue for meetings of volunteer soldiers, Methodist circuits and Poor Law unions, circus performances, temperance rallies and hiring fairs. An indication of the prosperity of Shropshire market towns is given by the table below. The population of the county increased by 45 per cent between 1801 and 1871. Some towns, like Bishop's Castle, Oswestry, Shrewsbury, Market Drayton and Church Stretton, exceeded this rate of growth. Others, including Ellesmere, Ludlow, Newport, Bridgnorth, Wem, Much Wenlock and Whitchurch, failed to match it. These figures mask some remarkable short-term changes. In the 1830s the population of Shrewsbury actually declined as a result of the closure of Benyons' flax mill and a falling-off of thorough-fare trade.

The Population of Shropshire Towns: 1801-1871

	Population in 1801	Population in 1871	Percentage increase
Bishop's Castle	1,076	1,805	68
Bridgnorth	4,408	5,876	33
Church Stretton	924	1,756	90
Cleobury Mortimer	1,368	1,708	24
Clun	794	1,029	29
Ellesmere	5,553	5,913	6
Ludlow	3,897	5,087	30
Market Drayton	3,162	4,844	53
Much Wenlock	1,981	2,531	28
Newport	2,307	3,202	38
Oswestry	2,672	7,306	173
Shifnal	3,642	6,681	83
Shrewsbury	14,739	23,406	59
Wem	3,087	3,880	26
Whitchurch	4,515	6,264	39
Shropshire	**170,000**	**248,000**	**45**
England and Wales	8,893,000	22,712,000	155

120 *A 19th-century market town. A view of Market Drayton from the south in 1824 (SJ675340).*

As in other counties country carriers brought to the towns passengers and produce from the rural areas and took back orders collected from the towns' shops. Their routes provide a means of analysing the influence of market towns. Shrewsbury was by far the most important market in Shropshire. In 1844, 87 carriers from 62 different villages made 181 calls a week in the town. Oswestry, with 29 carriers from 19 villages making 46 calls a week in 1851, was the only other town with significant numbers of carriers. Bridgnorth, Ludlow, Newport, Market Drayton and Whitchurch all had less than 20 services a week. Before the coming of the railway Shrewsbury was the market centre for a stretch of Welsh territory, extending some 70-80 miles to the coast at Towyn and Aberystwyth. Carrying from places served by direct trains declined as railways were opened, but services from other villages increased and as late as 1899 there were still 91 carriers from 70 different villages making 135 calls a week in Shrewsbury.

In the 19th century the principal shopkeepers in the market towns lived above their premises, often with their apprentices and assistants. A typical Shrewsbury shopkeeper's household was that of Maurice Jones, draper in Mardol, who in 1851 lived above his shop with his wife, four children and a niece, two assistants, two apprentices and a domestic servant. In Waterloo Terrace, Bridgnorth, in 1861, 11 people lived in the home of Thomas Knittam, draper, including six assistants and two domestic servants. In 1871 the household of John Valentine at 3-6 Broad Street, Ludlow, comprised 22 people, including his seven children, four domestic servants, two assistants in the Post Office, two grocer's assistants and four apprentices.

Shrewsbury was the only town to see the development of shops which were in any sense department stores. The shops of Maddox, Grocott and Della Porta, all grouped around the Square, offered a quality of shopping by the end of the 19th century that was unmatched elsewhere in the county.

121 *Mardol Head, Shrewsbury, painted by T.S. Boys in 1852, some 14 years before the buildings were demolished to make way for the new market hall. To the right, on the corner of Claremont Street (then Dog Row), is what must have been one of the tallest timber-framed buildings in Shrewsbury. The building at the rear of the jettied house, on which Boys's own sign is displayed, was even taller and appears to have had at least six storeys (SJ491125).*

New public buildings were erected in most Shropshire towns in the 19th century. Ellesmere's dramatic town hall dates from 1833. The Powis and Cross Markets in Oswestry were opened in 1849, and the Victoria Rooms in 1862. Much Wenlock Corn Exchange was built in 1882 and Newport's Italianate town hall in 1860. In 1869, market facilities in Shrewsbury were concentrated in a new building between Claremont Street and Shoplatch, the construction of which displaced more than 50 houses and over 300 people. A new market hall in the Italianate style to the design of Robert Griffiths of Quatford was built in Bridgnorth in 1856, but although the police tried to force traders to move into it, they resisted, and their successors continue to do business in the High Street every Saturday morning. Cattle markets were gradually moved from the streets into enclosed premises, which in Shropshire were often called Smithfields. The example was set by Shrewsbury where the cattle market moved in 1850 from the streets to premises off the newly-completed Smithfield Road.

The economies of the Shropshire market towns had much in common. All had drapers, grocers and ironmongers, large numbers of shoemakers, tailors and inns, with several solicitors' offices and at least one branch of a bank. Almost every town had at least one tanner—that of Charles McMichael in Bridgnorth employed 20 men and three boys in 1861. Most towns had a woolstapler, and all had maltsters. In 1851 there were 20 in Bridgnorth, 29 in Shrewsbury and 17 in Oswestry. In the 1880s and '90s the firm of William Jones & Son came to dominate Shropshire's malting trade. Bridgnorth, Ludlow, Market Drayton, Newport, Oswestry, Wellington and Shrewsbury had iron foundries producing agricultural implements. Carpets were made in Bridgnorth, gloves in Ludlow, bedding in Oswestry and horsehair in Market Drayton, while the manufacture of linen thread and yarn in Shrewsbury provided work for several hundred people until 1886. One of the county's best known minor industries was in Whitchurch, where J.B. Joyce & Co. produced clocks for all the stations on the London & North Western Railway.

The towns which prospered in the 19th century were all served by railways. Recollections of the Bishop's Castle branch show that railways were used for traffic over very short distances, such as the carriage of cattle bought by butchers at Craven Arms market to Bishop's Castle. In some towns the physical impact of railway construction was severe. The deep cutting in which the line passed through Wellington isolated the parish church from the town centre, and in Shrewsbury the building of the station caused the demolition of one side of Howard Street and of houses on Castle

122 *A cheese fair in Whitchurch, c.1910.*

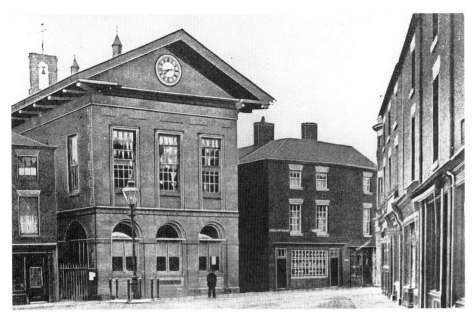

123 *The town hall at Ellesmere, opened in 1833 (SJ398348).*

124 *The Victoria Rooms at Oswestry (SJ292292), dating from 1862, was one of the largest places of public _assembly built in the market towns of Shropshire in the 19th century.*

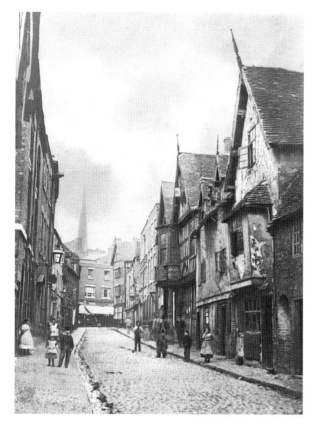

Hill, displacing several hundred people as well as destroying the open space between the prison and the castle. The town most affected by railways was Oswestry, headquarters of the Cambrian Railways and the centre for the construction and repair of the company's rolling stock. Its population grew by 35 per cent in the 1860s and by 173 per cent between 1801 and 1871, the fastest rate of growth of any town in the county. With its hundreds of terraced houses of the late 19th century, it remains the most Victorian of Shropshire towns. Craven Arms grew into a small town owing its existence to the railway, and taking its name from an 18th-century crossroads inn. It still has something of the atmosphere of a frontier settlement.

Most Shropshire towns served as 'open villages' for the surrounding estate parishes, places where labourers lived, often in overcrowded conditions, and walked daily into the countryside to their work. Most towns also had concentrations of masons, bricklayers and carpenters who earned their livings in the nearby villages. Bishop's Castle was notoriously overcrowded, and its rapid rate of growth was due not to the prosperity of its traders but to the clearance of cottages in the surrounding parishes. In 1865 Newport was described as 'an open village of the worst sort' from which workers walked out daily to farms, 20 men and 20 women a day trudging the four miles to and from Tibberton. Wenlock was said to be 'but a large open village' whose rough limestone cottages were densely overcrowded.

125 Above left. *Jacobean splendour and Victorian squalor. Claremont Street, Shrewsbury (SJ490125), c.1866 before the right-hand side was demolished to make way for the new market hall. In the centre is the* King's Arms, *a once-distinguished house, constructed in 1615, which became a hostelry in 1780. Several frescoes were discovered during its demolition.*

126 Above right. *The devastation caused by the demolition of Shoplatch and Claremont Street, Shrewsbury, in 1866, prior to the erection of the market hall (SJ490125).*

127 *Shrewsbury's Victorian market hall, designed by Robert Griffith (SJ490125), opened in 1869, and was demolished in the early 1960s.*

128 *Shrewsbury's Smithfield (SJ493127) in its last decade of operation in the 1950s. The cattle market was established in 1850, before which it had been held in the streets, and transferred to Harlescott in the early 1960s. The site is now occupied by car parks and shopping centres.*

129 *The butter market on Pride Hill, Shrewsbury (SJ493125) built in 1844. It closed after the opening of the market hall in 1869. From a print by Henry Blunt, c.1850.*

130 *The Butter Market, Howard Street, Shrewsbury (SJ494131), opened as a wholesale market for dairy produce when Shrewsbury was linked to the national canal network in 1835. It became the property of the London & North Western Railway, who, when it ceased to be used as a market after 1869, used it as a warehouse. After a spell of disuse from the 1960s, much evident in this photograph of 1982, it was adapted as a night club and concert hall in the mid-1980s.*

131 *Oswestry, Shropshire's most Victorian market town. The railway to the right is the ex-GWR branch from Gobowen, while that on the left is the Oswestry, Ellesmere & Whitchurch section of the Cambrian Railways, whose locomotive works stand to the left of it. In the fork between the two lines is the locomotive running shed (SJ295299).*

132 *Two of the terraces built in the vicinity of St Chad's Church, Shrewsbury (SJ488127), in the 1790s, when the town had some pretensions as a place of resort. John Carline and John Tilley designed Claremont Buildings, the terrace on the right, while the houses on the left may be the work of Thomas Telford.*

Some Shropshire towns had pretensions as places of resort, with houses designed to attract people who would settle and spend money rather than try to make it by trading. In the 1790s it was hoped that Shrewsbury might develop in this way but, although many annuitants and fundholders lived in the streets near St Chad's church in the mid-19th century, most were members of old Shrewsbury families rather than new arrivals. In 1810 a pamphleteer had urged Ludlovians to erect fine terraces on Whitecliffe, to build assembly rooms, to improve public walks and use local spring water, salt and coal to provide hot saline baths. By the middle of the 19th century Ludlow and Bridgnorth were attracting some families of the kind who normally settled in resorts. In 1851 John Penny, proprietor of houses, of land and a fundholder, was living in Dinham, Ludlow, with his wife, seven children and five servants. Ironically, he had been born in Bath, the prototype resort town. In 1861 the occupants of East Castle Street, Bridgnorth, included a retired Indian Army colonel with a daughter, born at Bangalore, at No. 17, and a surgeon from the Indian Army at No. 26. Another resort was the spa village of Admaston which was developed by a succession of enthusiastic owners of the spa hotel. In 1845 lists were published of families arriving to take the waters, and resident guests in 1861 included a clergyman, a civil engineer, a newspaper editor and a surgeon from the East India Service. The salubrious air, the excellent waters and the romantic situation of Church Stretton were already making it something of a resort by 1851, although it was best known at that time for its large private lunatic asylum. By the end of the century it was nationally celebrated as a resort, due to the enterprise of the Rev. Holland Sandford, vicar of Eaton under Heywood, who was responsible for laying out Sandford Avenue in 1884.

133 *W. Rogers and Son, millers and corn merchants, were established in Market Drayton in 1855.*

The towns served as centres for traditional entertainments. Many people went to Ludlow for the annual tug of war on Shrove Tuesday between the Castle and Broad Street and the Old and Corve Street wards. At Bridgnorth May Fair in 1864 it was noted that while the may bough was still cut on May Morning in the woods and coppices of Shropshire, May fairs in towns were held more for pleasure than business. The fair in Bridgnorth included gingerbread stalls, vendors of toys, swingboats, clowns and musicians. It was 'a real holiday; a day more than any other in the whole year on which the agricultural labourer feels himself free and unfettered'. Fairs provided occasions when young people could meet members of the opposite sex from communities other than their own. A writer in 1828 noted that 'At Ludlow ... the beauties of Herefordshire and Shropshire meet together in hilarity and display their rival beauties to the admiring swains; the land of cider and the land of beef send their sons hither'; while at Ellesmere 'the rosiest maidens in all the country round make havoc among the hearts of the likeliest swains in England'.

The old Shrewsbury Show on the Monday after Corpus Christi began with a parade of the trade guilds to Kingsland, where each guild had a booth which formed the centre for eating, drinking and dancing for its members. Burlesque figures with big comic heads led most of the guilds; Crispin and Crispianus with the shoemakers, Vulcan with the smiths, Sir Peter Paul Rubens with the house painters, Cupid and the Stag with the tailors and skinners, Henry VIII with the builders, Katherine of Aragon with the flax dressers and the Black Prince with the cabinet makers and hatters. In the early 19th century the show was thought to be in irremediable decline, but there was a revival in the 1840s, and in the '50s the railways brought vast numbers to see it. In 1853, 32,000 passengers arrived on special trains on Show Monday. As it grew in size it became more of a nuisance, and it was abolished in 1878, its cessation being a necessary precondition for the suburban development of Kingsland and the relocation of Shrewsbury School.

Race meetings attracted large crowds to the towns, as did circuses, theatrical performances and lectures by public figures like George Dawson and Henry Vincent. Shrewsbury was large enough to attract the most prestigious entertainments. In August 1858 Charles Dickens gave readings from *A Christmas Carol* in the Music Hall, where the following February Phineas T. Barnum expounded on 'The Science of Money-Making'. In 1886 *Tom Thumb* was brought to the town. The temperance movement in Shrewsbury was nationally celebrated owing to the leadership of Julia Wightman, wife of the vicar of St Alkmunds, who was responsible for the building of the Working Men's Hall in the Square in 1863, and for organising excursions to the Wrekin and Llangollen to take members of her society away from the temptations of Show Monday. In the 1880s, as the character of the Temperance Movement changed, five temperance coffee houses were built in Shrewsbury, but Mrs. Wightman had little sympathy for the new style of the movement.

The Olympian Games, held in Much Wenlock from 1850 onwards, were organised by William Penny Brookes, a native of the town who settled

134 *Ellesmere Town Hall, built in 1833.*

there after qualifying as a doctor in 1831. He was involved in many attempts to revitalise Wenlock's economy, the building of the corn exchange, of a gasworks, and of the local railway. The games were at first of a rustic character, with blindfold wheelbarrow races, and old women racing for pounds of tea, but gradually more track and field events were introduced and by 1870 notable athletes from all over Britain were competing. Winners were presented with olive crowns and medals and odes were declaimed in their honour. Baron de Coubertin, who organised the first modern Olympic Games in Athens in 1896, visited Much Wenlock in 1890 and wrote:

> ... and of the Olympic Games which modern Greece has not yet revived, it is not a Greek to whom one is indebted, but to Dr. W.P. Brookes ... now aged 82 ... still active and vigorous, organising and animating them ... Athletics does not count many partisans as convinced as W.P. Brookes.

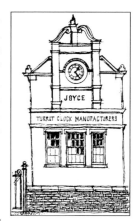

135 *The factory of J.B. Joyce & Co at Whitchurch.*

Professional football developed in the county in the closing decades of the 19th century. Shrewsbury Town Football Club was established in 1886, and the team's first games were played on Amblers Field on the opposite side of Monkmoor Road from the racecourse. For the 1902-03 season the club moved to Copthorne where the ground was situated between the present numbers 109 and 135 Copthorne Road. Eight years later the club moved to its present Gay Meadow ground where the first match was played on 10 September 1910.

Living conditions in some parts of most Shropshire towns were squalid. In Shrewsbury 158 deaths were caused by cholera in 1832 and 75 in 1849. Brothels flourished in areas like the Cartway in Bridgnorth and in Roushill in Shrewsbury, where there were more than 50 prostitutes in residence in 1861. An Improvement Commission in Shrewsbury in the 1820s removed such encroachments as flights of steps and bootscrapers from the streets, rounded many corners and began a street cleaning service, but in many areas squalor remained. Most Shropshire towns were lit by gas by the middle of the 19th century, and in subsequent decades sewers and piped water supplies were provided.

Brickyards and gravel pits were to be found on the outskirts of most Shropshire towns in the 19th century and many suburban houses were built of locally-quarried materials. In Belle Vue and in St Michael's Street, Shrewsbury and in New Road, Ludlow, there are extensive traces of brick clay quarries. Freehold Land Societies, which raised money from shareholders to buy land and then divided that land into building plots which were distributed among members, existed in Bridgnorth and Ludlow, and made a substantial contribution to the growth of Shrewsbury. The first Freehold Land Society estate in the county town, now Albert Street, Victoria Street and the south side of Severn Street, was built on the gardens behind the prison in the early 1850s. After the relocation of Shrewsbury School in 1882, the opening of Kingsland Bridge, and the closure of the old Shrewsbury Show, large-scale development of villas commenced on Kingsland, along three streets laid out with leasehold plots by the Corporation. Building materials were supplied from brickyards off the Copthorne Road by a tramway. The High Victorian suburb remains one of the best-conserved of

136 *The rounded corner at the junction of Pride Hill and High Street in Shrewsbury.*

its kind in Britain. A suburb of a different character was Rock Lane in Ludlow, the equivalent of Mixen Lane in Hardy's Casterbridge, where horsebreakers, washerwomen, hawkers of earthenware, basket makers, grinders of cutlery and brickmakers lived in roughly-built cottages along a much-braided thoroughfare, a community which was the precise antithesis of that which dwelt with such elegance in Broad Street and Mill Street. Similar rough suburbs were Bernard's Hill in Bridgnorth, and the Park Lane area of Shifnal.

Suburban pleasure grounds prospered on the edges of several towns. The *Beehive* public house on Kingsland was the main focus of Shrewsbury Show, and there was a tea garden at Underdale in the 1830s, which became the *Pineapple* public house in the 1840s. By the 1880s facilities were provided there for cycling, athletics, football, cricket and shooting. The Garland Tea Gardens in Sandpits Road, Ludlow, became a market garden and was then used for housing. On the outskirts of Wellington the *Forest Glen* became celebrated around 1900 as the starting point for ascents of the Wrekin.

Market towns in Shropshire were places of passage, the points at which people from the outside world made contacts with Salopians, and an examination of the lodging-houses of the mid-19th century poses many fascinating questions. In Bridgnorth in 1853 it was estimated that there were 28 lodging houses, and that a night's accommodation could be had for between fourpence and sixpence. In Newport in 1851 one of the tiny houses in Bellman's Yard was occupied by 23 and another by 25 Irish. In Shrewsbury 28 Irish lived in the house of Anthony Mallory, hawker, in St Michael's Street. Even in such a remote town as Bishop's Castle in 1851 there were Irish gatherers of rags and bones. In 1861 there were four carriers and a waggoner 'on travel' staying at the *Mitre Inn*, Ludlow, and five clogmakers from Lancashire at the nearby *Raven*. The most astonishing lodging house in the county was No. 18 Hills Lane, Shrewsbury, where in 1861 there were two pedlars, a hawker, a Welsh tailor, a drover from Somerset, an Irish army pensioner, two carpet weavers, a plate engraver and Asam Ali, a 44-year-old vendor of tracts born in the City of Mecca, Arabia, with his wife who was born in Cork.

137 *The Victoria Works, Oswestry, a typical market-town foundry which made agricultural machinery.*

17

The Victorian Countryside

Victorian Shropshire was overwhelmingly an agricultural county. The census for 1881 shows that the total population was 248,000, of whom 5,566 were farmers, and that there were 21,142 other agricultural workers, excluding those employed in forestry and horticulture. The only rural industries were stone quarries, some limeworks and brickyards, a few country tanneries and paper mills and many water corn mills. Nevertheless industry within the county, in the Coalbrookdale, Wyre Forest and Oswestry coalfields and the Stiperstones lead-mining region, and beyond its borders in Lancashire and the Black Country did offer alternative employment to country-dwellers, and farmworkers' wages in Victorian Shropshire were not as depressed as those in some counties in southern England.

138 *The great hall at Adcote.*

The main stimulus to agricultural improvement came from the great estates, and particularly from those of the Dukes of Sutherland centred on Lilleshall. In 1812 James Loch was appointed steward of the estates and, amidst his many activities on behalf of the Leveson Gower family, he supervised a rationalisation of farming on the Lilleshall estate. Roads and field boundaries were altered, farmhouses were rebuilt, new cottages in a distinctive estate style were constructed for labourers, and logically planned groups of barns, cow stalls and waggon sheds were designed, which remained models of their kind in the 1870s. Other estates were also in the vanguard of agricultural practice. Mechanisation of farming proceeded slowly. In the 1850s it was reckoned that only a few modern implements could be found on Shropshire farms, and that some wooden ploughs could still be seen in use. In the 1850s Thomas Drury of Prees was making his living by hiring out threshing machines, both steam- and horse-powered.

The enclosure of waste land continued during the 19th century. Between 1815 and 1891, 35 enclosure Acts were passed relating to land in Shropshire. Most were concerned with the uplands, like the Acts for Church Stretton in 1822, Clun Forest in 1845 and 1847, and Bettwys-y-crwyn in 1865, but some related to wetlands like the Act for the Weald Moors, passed in 1800 but only implemented in the early 1830s, and that for Whixall Moss, passed in 1823. The landscape of parliamentary enclosure, logically planned fields with regular boundaries, marked by quickset hedges, lining straight roads with uniform verges, can be observed on Cound Moor, on Clun Forest and alongside the Bridgnorth-Stourbridge turnpike road as it passes through the fields enclosed in the late 18th century from Morfe Common in the parish of Worfield.

Many of Shropshire's country houses remained the centres of miniature kingdoms, although several were threatened by the spendthrift habits of their owners, and some remained unoccupied for lengthy spells. Lilleshall Hall, built in a rather dour Gothic style by Sir Jeffry Wyatville in 1829, was only one of the four principal homes of the Dukes of Sutherland. The 1871 census shows Anne, Duchess of Sutherland in residence at Lilleshall, with two of her daughters, five visitors, four visitors' servants and 26 resident servants. In addition nine grooms and postilions lived in accommodation at the stables. Few other mansions had servants on quite this scale.

Most of the new country houses built in Shropshire during the 19th century were constructed for successful entrepreneurs. The Quinta, a Gothic house near Weston Rhyn, was built for Thomas Barnes, chairman of the Lancashire & Yorkshire Railway. It was one of the most self-sufficient of Victorian country houses, with a fire station and a gas works, and a series of sinuous drives designed to give the illusion that the grounds were larger than they actually were. The most distinguished of the Victorian country houses is Shropshire is Adcote, built by Richard Norman Shaw in 1876-79 for Rebecca, widow of Alfred Darby of Coalbrookdale. Shaw used the forms of 15th- and 16th-century English Gothic to produce a house which is full of unexpected vistas. If Adcote is the most subtle of Victorian mansions in Shropshire, Bedstone Court is the most spectacular. In 1880 the Bedstone estate was sold to Sir Henry Ripley, MP, grandson of the founder of the Bowling Dye Works in Bradford. Ripley commissioned Thomas Harris, author of *Victorian Architecture*, to build a vast house in the 'Old English Important Style'. It was a calendar house, with 12 chimneys, 365 windows,

139 *Bedstone Court (S0367755), designed in the 'Old English Important' style of Thomas Harrison for Sir Henry Ripley and built in the early 1880s.*

seven exterior doors and 52 rooms. Ventilation was by closable vents in the walls with a complex system of ducting. The house was lit by electricity and the plumbing on the upper floor was by an unusual system of rubber hoses. Bedstone Court was lavishly furnished with pre-Raphaelite paintings, Persian rugs, a walnut grand piano, Italian leather work, elaborate mosaics and an orchestrion in a glass case under the stairs. The Ripley family lived at Bedstone Court only until 1903.

One of the most significant distinctions in rural areas in the 19th century was that between the 'closed' villages, controlled by great estates or resident squires, and the 'open' villages, where most of the property was owned by small freeholders. Until 1865 each parish was responsible for raising by rates the costs of maintaining its own poor, and landowners who owned large parts of parishes had strong incentives to ensure that as few people as possible who were likely to become paupers gained settlements on their property. Only workers absolutely necessary for the operation of farms and estates were allowed to live in such parishes. Others came in each day from nearby 'open' villages where no such restrictions applied. Landowners in closed villages would often demolish cottages when they were vacated. Census returns between 1831 and 1871 refer to the demolition of cottages in Ditton Priors, Eaton-under-Heywood, Moreton Say, Pitchford, Neen Sollars, Upton Magna, Diddlebury, Munslow, Hopton Castle, Lee Brockhurst and Stoke-on-Tern. A few model dwellings were built in closed villages. In 1870 cottages designed by the London architect John Birch were constructed on the Dudmaston estate and at Caynham Court, each with a living room, scullery and pantry, three bedrooms, an entrance porch, a piggery, privy and fuel store. The showplaces of the period were the cottages built by Sir Baldwin Leighton on his Alberbury estate. They had only two bedrooms, and a kitchen and a larder on the ground floor, but tenants were encouraged to cultivate thrift with the prospect of being able to move to a cottage with land for a cow attached to it.

Many regularly-hired labourers travelled daily to their work from open villages and market towns, and in many parishes there were relatively few farm labourers who were heads of households. Some labourers were 'indoor' servants, staying in the households of their employers. It was usual for boys to be hired and to live in their masters' farmhouses from the age of 12 or 13 just as it was customary for their sisters to leave home for domestic service at that age. One farmer of 300 acres at Myddle in 1860 had five farm labourers living in his own house and three in cottages attached to the farm. At Ranslet Farm, Eaton Constantine, in 1851, Zachariah Smith employed six labourers on his 227 acres, of whom three lived in the farmhouse. Thomas Wilson of Cranmere, Worfield, in 1861 employed five men and a boy on his 312 acres, of whom two, a 16-year-old waggoner and a 26-year-old groom, lived in the farmhouse. An analysis of the labourers of Richards Castle parish suggests that the practice of living-in began to diminish in the 1860s. In 1841, 39.8 per cent of farm labourers were indoor servants, a proportion which fell to 35.6 per cent in 1851 and rose to 41.9 per cent in 1861, changes which are scarcely significant. The proportion fell sharply to 15.8 per cent in 1871.

140 *A smallholding at Weston Heath on the Sutherland estate.*

At harvest and haymaking periods Shropshire farmers often hired migrant Irish and Welsh workers. In 1827 John Barnett of Leighton hired six Welsh reaping men from near Llanfyllin in Montgomeryshire to gather his harvest at a cost of 6s. per acre. Women worked on most Shropshire farms, but not on a regular basis, so that census returns give an inadequate picture of their rôle. In 1827 John Barnett was paying a woman 8d. a day for weeding and for haymaking.

Some Shropshire clergy, among them the Rev. E. Jackson of Easthope, and the Rev. G.W. Pigott of Upton Magna, were pioneers in substituting harvest festival church services for traditional harvest homes. The latter were rarely village celebrations in Shropshire, but took place in farmers' homes, their effect being, according to their critics, to demoralise male workers and place before females 'scenes which it is painful to contemplate'. The harvest festival at Upton Magna in 1857 consisted of a church service, followed by lunch on the rectory lawn accompanied by a band from Shrewsbury, toasts to the landlord, Robert Burton, a cricket match, races, and afternoon tea at five o'clock.

A government enquiry carried out in 1869 found that labourers' cottages in Shropshire were worse than in any other English county except Dorset. The schoolmaster at Clun told the enquiry that half of his pupils belonged to families living in houses with only one bedroom. Few cottages of this period survive to be studied, and it seems that a real shortage of agricultural labour became evident in the closing years of the 19th century, when older dwellings were demolished and replaced by the many cottages of that period which can still be seen. The process of squatting continued well into the 19th century. On Pontesbury Hill over 100 cottages were built between 1785 and the enclosure of the area in 1848. Many were originally turf huts and had been converted into stone cottages by the late 1850s.

The administration of the Poor Law in Shropshire was radically reorganised in 1836-37, in accordance with the 1834 Poor Law Amendment Act, by William Day, as assistant Poor Law Commissioner. Responsibility for the administration of relief was transferred from the parishes to unions of parishes, governed by boards of elected guardians. The six unions of parishes established in the 1780s and '90s all continued, which made the pattern of the new unions less logical than it might otherwise have been. Under the chairmanship of Sir Baldwin Leighton from 1836 to 1871, the Atcham Union, which encircled Shrewsbury, gained a reputation as the 'best-run' union in England. The main principal of the 1834 Act, that the able-bodied should only be relieved within the workhouse, was fiercely applied. By contrast outdoor relief was liberally provided in the Shrewsbury parishes until they were merged with Atcham in 1871. Few landed gentlemen in England did more than Sir Baldwin Leighton to instil into the labouring classes a dread and hatred of the workhouse. He treated his own staff with the same disdain which he displayed to those whose poverty drove them to seek sustenance from public funds. When in 1855 he found that his gamekeeper had taken home two rabbits, he insisted that he should be tried at the Assize, but Lord Campbell, who was presiding at the court, imposed a nominal sentence, and suggested that if Sir Baldwin wished to deny perquisites to his staff, he should simply have dismissed the man and saved the expense of a trial.

Universal primary education came slowly to Shropshire. Village schools were established in some parishes well before 1850, and many more were built following the 1870 Education Act and the measure of 1876 which made schooling compulsory. Reports by Her Majesty's Inspectors reveal a steady increase in standards, in spite of adverse social conditions. 'The conspicuous defect in this school', wrote one exasperated HMI of the Bog School in Wentnor parish in 1898, 'is the lack of intelligence shown by the children.' Some farmers thought that education destroyed the willingness of labourers' sons to follow their fathers on to the land. One said in 1867 that 'Farmers did not want to have their plough boys and farm labourers taught to read and write. They did very well as they were, and if they were sent to school they might have them turn round upon the farmers.' Many labourers objected that their sons were kept in school instead of going out to contribute to the family income, and the payment of school pence was often resisted. Log books from schools in all parts of Shropshire suggest that attendance regulations in the 19th century were laxly administered or simply proved unenforceable, but by 1900 attendances were improving.

The life of a child growing up in rural Shropshire in the 1860s or '70s was dominated by the demands of agriculture. At certain seasons a child as young as six would either be working or minding younger children while his mother worked. At Bishop's Castle boys were often absent from school on market days when they could find employment minding cattle. Haymaking, harvest and potato setting and gathering demanded the help of all available hands. In 1868 a large crop of acorns coincided with a shortage of feeding grains, and all over Shropshire children were kept away from school to collect acorns for feeding to pigs. A waggoner's family from Lydbury North collected five bushels of wheat by gleaning in the autumn of 1868. Around the Stiperstones and the Long Mynd, school holidays began when the whimberries were ripe, and the children did not return to school until there were no more berries to pick. At the Bog School in 1893 the summer holiday began as early as 16 June because the whimberries had ripened exceptionally early. Whimberry buyers in the Clun area usually paid out £500, and sometimes as much as £800 a year. In woodland areas bark peeling for the market town tanneries occupied children for long periods.

141 *Richard Norman Shaw's village school of 1872 at Church Preen (SO555975).*

142 *The creamery at Pipe Gate, Woore, on the Staffordshire border (SJ737408), flourished in the 1920s and '30s, and is now a rubber factory.*

143 *A label used for one of the products of Minsterley Creamery in the 1930s.*

Emigration to Australia, North America and elsewhere was little by little, changing the nature of rural society in Shropshire. There were no large-scale and well-publicised emigration projects in Shropshire, but recent research suggests that the outflow of migrants throughout the 19th century was considerable. Newspapers carried numerous advertisements from shipping companies offering passages to Australia or North America, and occasionally printed lengthy accounts from migrants of their experiences. The *Shrewsbury Chronicle* in 1859 included several letters from William Storey of Shrewsbury, who sailed to Adelaide in the sailing ship *Libertas* and was delighted that the city was so 'English-like'. In the 1890s and until the outbreak of the First World War the Canadian government supported the work of emigration agents in Shropshire, most notably Walter Rumsey of Shrewsbury, who ensured a steady flow of agricultural labourers to the prairie provinces.

Shropshire, with its many dairy and sheep farms, was less affected by the Agricultural Depression of the late 19th century than regions where there was more arable cultivation, although the county suffered as much as any other from the succession of wet seasons, the foot and mouth epidemics and other disasters of the late 1870s and early '80s. Grain crops became less important, and new implements and new crops were adopted. Creameries were built, like that at Minsterley, which began work in 1906. It supplied milk for distribution in Birmingham, and made cheese when milk was over-plentiful.

By the end of the century the rural community was becoming more unified. The Shropshire Chamber of Agriculture formed in 1866 provided a county-wide forum for farming interests, and the Shropshire branch of the National Farmers' Union was founded in 1908. In 1875 the first West Midland Show was held in the Quarry in Shrewsbury. The show became an annual focus for the social life of the agricultural community, many schools giving holidays to allow children to attend. Agricultural education also proved a unifying factor. In 1892 Thomas Harper Adams, a farmer from Edgmond, died leaving £37,000 with 178 acres of land as an endowment for an agricultural college, which opened with the support of the Shropshire and Staffordshire county councils in 1901. In the same year Radbrook College opened at Shrewsbury to provide girls from rural areas with training in domestic science and dairy work. Whatever the difficulties posed by the Depression, the agricultural community was becoming better educated and less isolated.

XIII *A tollhouse on the Oswestry turnpike road network at Porthywaen (SJ258235).*

XIV *Penyllan Mill near Oswestry (SJ278281). In spite of the presence of a tall 19th-century chimney, the mill machinery was always worked by water-power, never by steam.*

XV *The Hoffman kiln (SJ267212), used for the production of lime at Llanymynech in the early years of the 20th century.*

XVI *The massive keep of Hopton Castle (S0367779), a stronghold of the Mortimer family in the 14th century. The castle gives its name to a small parish of just over 2,000 acres.*

18

Into the 20th Century

The Local Government Acts of 1888 and 1894 created a system of admin-istration in Shropshire which lasted with minor alterations for over eighty years. The new Salop County Council assumed many of the responsibilities of the former Quarter Sessions, and the landed gentlemen who had been prominent in Quarter Sessions led the new body as chairmen of committees. Few elections to the new council were contested. The first working-class councillor, a miner, was elected in 1907, and the first woman in 1922. Political controversy was avoided where possible, and the ability to conciliate was the most admired attribute of council leaders. The County Council took over the responsibilities of many of the *ad hoc* local government bodies which had been set up in the 19th century. The 1902 Education Act gave it responsibility for schools, and in 1930 it inherited the duties of the Poor Law guardians. There were 33 central staff in 1907, and only 77 in 1924. None of the council's leading members was an advocate of large-scale public spending. The council's most notable early achievement was in secondary education. Between 1909 and 1914, 13 new secondary schools were estab-lished, as a result of which the rate of admissions to universities from schools in Shropshire in the 1920s was higher than the national average.

144 *Shropshire Yeo-manry Cavalry badge.*

The reforms of the 1890s created a second tier of local government which consisted of 17 rural districts, nine urban districts and six municipal boroughs, which included the borough of Wenlock which comprised large tracts of agricultural countryside and the southern portion of the Coalbrookdale coalfield, and Bishop's Castle, which, with a population of under 2,000, prided itself on being the smallest borough in England. In many respects the boundaries of the new authorities followed those of the Poor Law unions established in 1834-37, which in some areas had been those of unions set up in the 1790s. Many of the new authorities were small. Whitchurch Rural District consisted of only two parishes, and Chirbury of three, and most lacked sufficient rate income to carry out their duties effectively. In 1934 the rural districts of Burford, Chirbury, Cleobury Mortimer, Newport, Church Stretton, Teme and Whitchurch were absorbed into neighbouring authorities. Parish councils, a lively part of the machinery of government in some parts of rural Shropshire, were established in 1894.

The First World War brought many changes. On the declaration of war thousands of Salopians thronged the recruiting offices. In the latter stages of the conflict, troops from the United States and Canada were

145 *A First World War prisoner-of-war camp alongside the Shrewsbury & Hereford Railway viaduct in Abbey Foregate, Shrewsbury (SJ49-8124). Three of the prisoners in the foreground appear to be German submariners.*

stationed in the county, while there was a conspicuous camp for German prisoners of war in Abbey Foregate, Shrewsbury. Military hospitals were established at Hatton Grange, Shifnal, and at Oakley Manor, Shrewsbury, the latter moving to Prestfelde in 1917. The Royal Flying Corps began to fly Sopwith Camels from Tern Hill in 1916, and the flying field at Shawbury came into operation the following year, although both were closed in the 1920s. At Monkmoor, Shrewsbury, a flying field was laid out early in 1918 which was used as an aircraft acceptance park and a school of reconnaissance. Women took up occupations previously regarded as male preserves. In the winter of 1917-18 female tractor drivers, trained at Harper Adams College, were in Manchester ploughing up Old Trafford racecourse for food production. The war affected even the remotest parts of Shropshire. The Bishop's Castle Railway enjoyed a period of prosperity as it carried thousands of tons of timber for the war effort.

The county regiment, the King's Shropshire Light Infantry, had been formed under Edward Cardwell's army reforms in 1881, its first battalion being the former 53rd of foot, and the second the former 85th. In wartime conditions the regiment was much enlarged. In the summer of 1914 the first battalion was in England and crossed to France on 10 September 1914. It suffered heavy casualties, in the first Battle of Ypres in the autumn, and then remained in the trenches around Ypres until August 1916, when it moved to the Somme, where it took part in the tank-led assault on Cambrai, and bore much of the brunt of the Ludendorff offensive in the early months of 1918. The second battalion was in India at the outbreak of war, but returned to Europe. After spells in the Ypres salient and on the Somme, the battalion went to Salonika where it arrived in the first week of December 1915, and remained in the region until the cessation of hostilities. The fourth battalion, consisting of men who had been in the Territorial Army before the war, was sent to the Far East in December 1914, where it remained until 1917, when it returned to fight at Passchendaele. The fifth battalion was raised from the first onrush of volunteers in response to Lord Kitchener's appeal in 1914, while the sixth was a 'pals' battalion, consisting entirely of men from Shrewsbury. Both spent most of the war on the Western Front, where in May 1916 four battalions of the regiment were involved in halting the German attack on Railway Wood near Ypres. The Shropshire Yeomanry spent the first 15 months of the war on the east coast before being converted to an infantry regiment. In the spring of 1916 they sailed to Alexandria, and served in Palestine before returning to play a distinguished part as the 10th battalion of the KSLI in the final stages of the conflict on the Western Front. The Salopian who is best remembered for his part in the First World War is Wilfred Owen, perhaps the most talented of the war poets. He was born near Oswestry in 1893, the son of a railway clerk who moved to Shrewsbury in 1907. Wilfred Owen attended the Technical College by the English Bridge and from 1913 to 1915 taught at a school in France. He returned to take a commission, and met his death a few days before the Armistice in 1918.

146 Hangars with Belfast truss roofs built by the Royal Air Force on the flying field at Monkmoor, Shrewsbury (SJ514136), in 1918. In the 1920s the hangars were used for a short time as a sports hall. They were re-occupied by the RAF during the Second World War and are now used for manufacturing and retailing.

One of the most significant changes in rural Shropshire in the post-war period was the sale of the Duke of Sutherland's Lilleshall estate in 1922. Lilleshall Hall became a pleasure park during the 1920s, advertised by the slogan 'See Lilleshall and know the thrill of living'. Many estate farms were sold to their tenants, most of whom continued the traditions of progressive farming established by James Loch. In spite of the depression which afflicted agriculture nationally, some estates continued to prosper. Under Geoffrey Wolryche Whitmore forestry work on the Dudmaston estate was skilfully revived, and in 1951 Dudmaston was chosen as a typical integrated estate to be portrayed at the Festival of Britain. The motor car and the charabanc

147 *The miniature railway which ran from Lilleshall Hall to the ruins of the Augustinian Priory of Lilleshall, when 'Lovely Lilleshall' was a pleasure park in the 1920s and '30s.*

stimulated the development of Ellesmere as a 'honeypot' for day trippers. In 1934 Lord Brownlow built a restaurant on the side of the mere, and provided boats for hire, but he became disillusioned with his investment when local magistrates refused to grant the restaurant a licence for the sale of alcoholic drinks. At Church Stretton the Chalet Pavilion in the Carding Mill Valley was being promoted in the 1920s as a suitable venue for outings for up to 300 people travelling in charabancs, which could drive up to the door.

In 1893 legislation permitted county councils to provide smallholdings for those who wished to establish themselves in farming, but in Shropshire this was not done until the Smallholdings and Allotments Act of 1907 made such provision compulsory. By 1913 the county council had provided 94 holdings totally 1,000 acres. After the First World War another 7,000 acres were obtained, so that by 1939 the county council had 380 holdings. The white-painted farmsteads at such places as Cruckton, Emstrey and Leebotwood have become familiar features of the Shropshire landscape. The scheme was profitable in the inter-war years, and there was never any shortage of capable applicants.

The other major development in agriculture in the inter-war years was the adoption of a new crop. With the backing of a consortium of Shropshire farmers and landowners, a sugar beet processing factory was constructed at Allscott in 1927, and many farmers subsequently grew beet in rotation with other crops. Creameries came to be major factors in the rural economy. New enterprises were set up at Ruyton-XI-Towns, Whittington, Whitchurch, Crudgington, amongst other places. At Ellesmere a creamery was established by George Stokes in 1919 in the one-time Bridgewater Foundry on the Canal Wharf. The first milk arrived in three churns in a cart driven by an ex-soldier who had been wounded on the western front. By the early 1930s the Ellesmere factory was famous for the quality of its cheese, and regularly dispatched liquid milk to London.

The pattern of industry in the county changed slowly. In 1901-2 the Simpson-Bibby steam waggon had been constructed at Horsehay, but large-scale production went ahead at the works of Alley & MacLellan at Polmadie, Glasgow. In 1915 the company sought a new site, and their manager George Woodvine, who had once worked at Horsehay, chose an area on the north side of Shrewsbury. Construction of a factory from components prefabricated in Glasgow began in March 1915, and the first waggon was finished in the summer of that year. A new company, the Sentinel Waggon Works Ltd., was formed in 1918. On the opposite side of the main road to Whitchurch the company built a hundred houses for their workpeople, with central heating, hot water and electric power supplied from the factory. During the inter-war period the Sentinel Works became celebrated for its steam lorries and for the high pressure, chain-drive equipment which it supplied for railway locomotives and railcars. Locomotives were exported to Canada, India, Sweden and South Africa, while railcars were supplied to Egypt, Malaya, Nigeria, Peru and Romania. The Castle Works at Hadley originated as a

148 *The Sentinel Waggon Works, Harlescott, Shrewsbury (SJ50-5147), in the 1920s with two waggons about to be despatched to customers.*

149 Left. *A cul-de-sac on the Sentinel Gardens estate adjacent to the Sentinel Waggon Works, Shrewsbury (SJ505146). This estate, designed on Garden City principles, was built c.1920 to accommodate workers making steam waggons.*

150 Left, below. *The original interior of a kitchen on the Sentinel Gardens estate.*

151 Left, below right. *One of the last steam lorries to be produced at the Sentinel Waggon Works. This S4 vehicle was completed in May 1937, just two months before lorry production ceased (although some were constructed for Argentina in 1950). This lorry worked for the Castle Firebrick Co of Buckley, Flintshire, until 1957, and was subsequently employed by Early Transport of Wareham, Dorset. It is now in private ownership in Shropshire.*

forge making wrought-iron, and in the early 20th century was used by George Milnes for the manufacture of tramcars. In 1910 it was taken over by John Sankey of Bilston to make pressed steel wheels and the following year began to make steel bodies for road vehicles. After wartime expansion, the works specialised in making chassis for the motor industry, and the factory became one of the growth points in the county. The Coalbrookdale Company reorganised its activities after becoming a subsidiary of Allied Ironfounders Ltd. in 1929, and installed the first completely mechanical moulding and sand conditioning plant in a British foundry. The activities of the Lilleshall Company contracted. Three collieries were closed, the Bessemer steel plant at Priorslee ceased to operate in 1922, Snedshill Forge closed in 1926 and in 1930-31 the heavy engineering works at the New yard, St George's was shut down.

152 Above. *Electricity comes to Ludlow. Cables being laid in 1906 at Castle Square for the Ludlow Electric Light Co. (SO509745).*

153 *Shropshire Canal, 1808.*

Electric power generation for public supply began in Shrewsbury and Oswestry in 1895, and further power stations were built at Market Drayton in 1902, Church Stretton in 1904, Ludlow in 1906 and Bishop's Castle in 1914. The West Midlands Joint Electricity Authority built a large new coal-fired power station at Ironbridge, opened on 13 October 1932. The Shropshire, Worcestershire & Staffordshire Power Co., formed in 1903, which built the Stourport power station in 1927, was a pioneer of rural electrification and acquired the undertakings at Church Stretton, Ludlow and Bishop's Castle.

Most of the county's canals fell out of use, and the more marginal branch railways were closed. At the same time the county council began to improve roads to meet the demands of motor traffic. There were complaints about the dust rising from unbonded surfaces as early as 1903 when there were only 125 motor cars in Shropshire. In 1911 the first tarred surfaces were laid. The county began a substantial programme of reconstruction and re-surfacing in 1925-26. In 1929 a concrete bridge was opened at Atcham to replace John Gwynn's 18th-century stone structure, which was fortunately left in position. The first by-pass in the county, avoiding a dangerous series of blind bends in the village of Gobowen, was completed in 1926. The Shrewsbury by-pass was opened in 1933, and by-passes were also provided for St George's and Church Stretton. These achievements were due largely to the forceful character of W.H. Butler, County Surveyor from 1924 to 1948. The Ministry of Transport took over from the County Council the administration of 118 miles of trunk roads in 1937. In the more thickly populated parts of the county omnibus proprietors competed fiercely in the 1920s. Most of the traffic was ultimately shared between the spheres of influence of the Midland Red company based in Shrewsbury, Wellington and Ludlow, and the Oswestry-based Crossville group, but in the coalfield a producers' co-operative, the Mid-Shropshire Omnibus Operators Association, was formed in 1930 to compete with the Midland Red on the routes from Wellington to Donnington and St George's.

154 *A stop lock on the Shropshire Canal, the last working section of which fell out of use in the early 20th century. The section through the Blists Hill Open Air Museum was restored in 1972-73.*

The General Strike in May 1926 was one of the most memorable incidents of the inter-war period, even in a largely rural county. In Shrewsbury striking railwaymen held prayer meetings each morning in the Primitive Methodist chapel, while in Oswestry they organised nightly concerts. The Co-operative Stores in Oswestry posted news of the strike on its windows. Manufacturing industry, much of it already on short time, was little affected, and towns like Bishop's Castle were reported to be 'nearly normal'. Lorries kept the county supplied with food from Liverpool docks. In Shrewsbury 1,500 enrolled as volunteer workers, and in the county as a whole 1,455 special constables were sworn in. The National Citizens' Union organised a programme of lifts, and boys were conveyed to Shrewsbury School for the start of term by a co-operative of parent car drivers. An ex-army officer driving a train at Craven Arms regretted that he was not allowed to go faster. Ellen Wilkinson spoke at a meeting in support of the strikers on the Quarry, Shrewsbury on Saturday 8 May. From time to time wild rumours spread round the county, like the claim made on 17-18 May that a striker

had been killed in a brawl with police at Oakengates. Loudspeakers relaying BBC broadcasts were set up at principal police stations to counter their effects. The General Strike ended without violence in Shropshire, but the miners' strike continued long afterwards.

The inter-war period saw much house-building in Shropshire, although the population was not increasing rapidly in the 1920s. There was a fall of rather less than one per cent between 1911 and 1931, but an increase of 18.7 per cent during the next two decades. Shrewsbury's population grew by 10.15 per cent between 1911 and 1931, while that of Ludlow fell by five per cent and that of the coalfield by three per cent. Between 1931 and 1951 Shrewsbury grew by 38 per cent, Ludlow by 14 per cent and the coalfield by 36 per cent. Local authorities became involved with the provision of housing after Lloyd George's promises in the 1918 general election to build homes fit for heroes. One of the first council housing schemes in Shrewsbury was in Longden Green, an area which was fully built up by 1927. Wellington RDC built 50 houses at Hadley under Christopher Addison's Housing Act of 1919, and a further 222 under the Housing Provision Act of 1924. Shrewsbury Borough Council cleared 100 families from slum dwellings and accommodated them in council houses between 1926 and 1933. Extensive new areas of private housing were also constructed. In Shrewsbury, Woodfield Road had just been laid out in housing plots at the time when the 1927 edition of the Ordnance Survey was prepared. In 1934 the Blackpool builders A. & G.R. Fletcher began to construct 130 houses on the site of

155 *Grasmere Road and Rydal Avenue, the first houses in Shrewsbury built by Messrs. A. & G.R. Fletcher in the mid-1930s, on the site of a disused RAF road transport base on the north side of Shrewsbury (SJ507155).*

156 *Shropshire Women's Institute badge.*

a disused RAF mechanical road transport depot at Harlescott. Some of the ex-RAF buildings were demolished and replaced with housing; others were developed as industrial premises. Before the outbreak of war in 1939 the firm had constructed about 450 houses in Shrewsbury, 80 in Whitchurch, 200 in Wellington and 14 in Dawley. A Fletcher house at Harlescott could be obtained for £495 freehold in 1934. A three-bedroomed 'Sunshine House' in Monkmoor Avenue could be purchased for £675 in 1936. Similar estates of semi-detached villas appeared at the edges of most towns in the county. Most were architecturally unremarkable although some in the Copthorne area of Shrewsbury show an awareness of the Modern Movement. The landscape of the coalfield remained grim, and unemployment was high. The Rev. J.E.G. Cartledge, vicar of Oakengates, organised a series of work camps from 1933 onwards, at which pit mounts were levelled to create sites for community use.

Several new county organisations grew up in the inter-war period. The first Young Farmers' Club in the county met at Newport in 1929. There were eight such clubs a decade later, and a county federation was formed in 1949. The first Women's Institute in Shropshire met at Edgmond in 1917. Nine institutes were formed during 1918, and there were more than fifty by 1923. The Shropshire Federation of Women's Institutes was formed in 1922. Many cinemas opened, some converted from other buildings and some purpose-built, reflecting the architectural taste of the times, like the Granada in Shrewsbury which was begun in 1934. Chain stores appeared in the streets of the principal market towns. F.W. Woolworth opened branches in Shrewsbury, Wellington, Ludlow, Bridgnorth and Oswestry. A popular attraction in Shrewsbury was the café on the first floor of Boots store in Pride Hill which offered 'Luxury with Economy: High-Class Luncheons and Teas at Popular Prices'. Many of Shrewsbury's finest timber buildings were destroyed, to be replaced for the most part by shops and offices in a bland neo-Georgian style.

Shropshire contained parts of all the three nations defined by J.B. Priestley in his *English Journey* of 1933, although Priestley did not include the county on his itinerary. The 'Old England' of churches, manor houses, inns and teashops could easily be located in Ludlow or Bridgnorth, although the sights sought by tourists masked a good deal of rural poverty. The 19th-century England of coal, iron and railways was to be found in the Coalbrookdale Coalfield and to a lesser extent around Oswestry. There were few parts of that England more depressed in the 1930s than Oakengates or Dawley. Shrewsbury, with its growing population, represented the third England of by-pass roads, cinemas, dance-halls, Woolworths and factories which looked like exhibition buildings. In none of these respects was Shropshire exceptional. The county suffered poverty caused by unemployment, but not on the scale of Tyneside or South Wales. It was visited by motor-borne tourists, but not by the numbers who flocked to the Cotswolds. It had modern factories but not like those of the Great West Road. The inter-war period was a quiet one in Shropshire's history and the county rarely attracted national attention.

19

The Second World War and After 1939-63

At 4.45 a.m. on 1 September 1939 German troops entered Poland, and two days later a reluctant British government declared war, marking the beginning of five years of social and economic upheaval. Thousands of Salopians travelled to the ends of the earth, while the market towns of Shropshire became social centres for servicemen from all parts of Britain, the Commonwealth, the United States and the occupied countries of Europe, and displaced persons from many countries worked on Shropshire farms.

The outbreak of war was not unexpected and government in Shropshire as elsewhere had detailed plans which were immediately implemented. Mechanical excavators dug trenches in the Quarry in Shrewsbury as a precaution against air raids, while in Bridgnorth children used their seaside spades to fill sandbags to protect the infirmary. Ludlow town hall was converted into a casualty clearing station. Gas masks were issued even in settlements as remote as Rhydycroesau. Fuel Overseers and Food Executive Officers were appointed, and War Agricultural Sub-Committees organised the ploughing up of grassland.

Plans to evacuate children from the conurbations were immediately put into effect, the reception of the refugees being organised by district councils. The Oakengates, Newport and Dawley urban districts were allocated children from Smethwick, but most of Shropshire took in refugees from Merseyside. The evacuation programme began on Friday 1 September and was largely completed within four days. Lengthy trains with main line stock and locomotives found their way along some of the more remote by-ways of the Shropshire railway system. Atcham district received its evacuees at Pontesbury station, where 750 children arrived at 3.30 p.m. on Sunday 3 September and a further 800 the following day. Four trains of evacuees from Liverpool travelled along the Severn Valley line to Bridgnorth, while 1,000 children from Birkenhead and Liverpool arrived at Oswestry. Some schools were moved to Shropshire and shared facilities with local educational institutions. Lancing College was accommodated at Moor Park in Richards Castle, Birkenhead Institute at Oswestry Boys High School and Notre Dame Collegiate School at Whitchurch High School. The evacuees' hosts were astonished by the poverty to which some of their guests had been accustomed. The staid inhabitants of Ludlow established a de-lousing station, and burned many soiled mattresses, and in Ironbridge, not the most prosperous part of Shropshire, many evacuees were considered to be dirty and ragged, and to have habits which the natives found filthy. Many evacuee children were soon taken back to their homes, but waves of them returned when bombing raids increased. At the Bog School on the Stiperstones five children were admitted during September 1939, but only one remained by the end of November.

A notable evacuee was Colonel (later General) Charles de Gaulle, who arrived in England on 13 June 1940. He and his wife arranged for their daughter to attend the Convent of Our Lady of Sion at Acton Burnell and, while de Gaulle was on the ill-fated expedition to Dakar in August 1940, his wife rented Gadlas Hall near Ellesmere. She remained there until the autumn of 1941, sought garlic, olive oil and gherkins from grocers in Ellesmere, and attended mass in a corrugated-iron scout hut. General de Gaulle returned to England on 17 November and began to travel to Gadlas every few weeks.

The first battalion of the KSLI crossed to France in September 1939. During the German offensive through Belgium in May 1940 the regiment retreated from Tournai to Dunkirk covering the last 40 miles on foot. The second battalion was in the West Indies, and it was not until February 1942 that they sailed to England. The first battalion landed in North Africa in March 1943. In December 1943 they joined the 8th Army in southern Italy, entered Rome on 4 June 1944, and after a period on the Gothic Line in the Apennines moved to the Middle East in February 1945. The second battalion trained in Scotland for the D-Day landings, crossed the Seine on 16 September 1944, made rapid progress through Belgium, fought in the Battle of Overloon, and wintered west of the Maas. They crossed the Rhine on 19 March 1945, and reached Minden on VE Day. The fourth, territorial battalion of the regiment trained in Northern Ireland after mobilisation, and moved to England late in 1941 to join the 159th Brigade, the lorry-borne infantry of the 11th Armoured Division. They landed in Normandy on 14 June 1944, were involved in the battle for Caen and the sealing of the Falaise Pocket, took part in the pursuit of the German army from the Seine to the Albert Canal, and achieved distinction in the fighting which dislodged the Nazis from Antwerp. They crossed the Rhine on 28 March 1945, captured Osnabruck on 3 April, and ended the war at Bad Oldesloe, east of the Elbe.

The Shropshire Yeomanry had remained through the inter-war period a traditional county cavalry regiment. On mobilisation the regiment assembled at Adderley Hall, which was then empty, and Shavington, the home of Major Arthur Heywood-Lonsdale, the second-in-command. 567 horses were purchased for the regiment's use, but in January 1940 the Yeomanry became the 75th and 76th Medium Regiments of the Royal Artillery. The 75th left Greenock in August 1942 for Port Tewfik in Egypt, from where they moved to Baghdad and Palestine, and crossed to Italy in December 1943. The 76th sailed to Port Tewfik in February 1943 before crossing to Sicily and then to the Italian mainland. Both regiments fought in the Apennines, the 75th ending the war on the River Po, and the 76th in Bologna.

By 1944 thousands of Salopians were scattered over the world in a variety of units. A REME staff sergeant from Shrewsbury sent home descriptions of a visit to a Tibetan temple, and a Much Wenlock soldier was reported to be in Nineveh. At the same time soldiers, airmen and naval personnel moved into bases in Shropshire. The greatest and most lasting change came at Donnington where the Woolwich Arsenal was re-located just before the outbreak of war. Between 1941 and 1943, 844 houses were built for the employees of the Ordnance Depot. Most bases in Shropshire were used for training and storage. The camps around Oswestry provided the first acquaintance with military life for thousands of army recruits. The Shropshire & Montgomeryshire Railway was brought back to life to serve as the communications lifeline for the Central Ammunition Storage Depot, Nesscliff, which comprised 2,000 acres of flat, damp, sparsely-populated countryside between Ford and Kinnerley. Ammunition of 1,502 different types arrived in wagons and was stored in buildings protected by huge earthen banks. The Ditherington Maltings in Shrewsbury, the first iron-framed building, was a training centre for army recruits.

The Royal Air Force moved into Shropshire in great numbers. There was a huge training depot at Stanmore, Bridgnorth, and 20 or so flying fields, most of them used for training, the reception of new aircraft and the repair of those damaged in combat. By 1939 the two First World War bases at Shawbury and Tern Hill had been reopened, and new bases had been built at High Ercall and Cosford. More airfields were constructed in the years 1940-42. The base which saw the most action was probably Peplow. Wellington bombers were based there from 1943 onwards, and aircraft burning on the ground at dawn after crash landings caused by damage during raids became a grimly familiar sight.

157 *The stable block at Shavington in the parish of Adderley, where the Shropshire Yeomanry assembled on the outbreak of the Second World War. The adjacent 17th-century mansion was demolished in the 1950s (SJ638387).*

The war even brought the Royal Navy to Shropshire. The Fleet Air Arm had its instrument flying school at Hinstock Hall and in 1939 the Admiralty began to store ammunition at Ditton Priors near the terminus of the Cleobury Mortimer & Ditton Priors Light Railway. During 1941 a depot was built on the site, and the once quiet railway backwater became busy with trains carrying torpedoes and shells.

St Dunstan's moved to Church Stretton as it had done during the First World War. Blind patients guided themselves along a system of wires between the town centre and the hospital's headquarters at the *Long Mynd Hotel*.

Manufacturing concerns went over to war work. The Lilleshall Company from 1940 until 1943 was making a million and a quarter bullet-proof rivets a month. The Horsehay Company manufactured steel landing craft, using a horse-drawn plateway to keep the erectors supplied with materials. The Sentinel Waggon Works built machine tools, Bren Gun carriers, landing ramps for the Normandy invasions and military refrigeration equipment.

Agriculture was transformed. In the first year of the war 47,000 extra acres in the county were ploughed up, and farmers were urged to use their grass for silage. In some villages, like Rhydycroesau, the first tractors appeared during the course of the war. Members of the Women's Land Army in their green jumpers and khaki hats and breeches worked on many farms, using houses like Burwarton Rectory as hostels. Soldiers and later Italian and German prisoners of war were set to work during haymaking and harvesting and by the end of the war hundreds of Shropshire school children were spending several weeks each autumn picking potatoes.

158 *Harvesting near Lilleshall in the late 1940s.*

Apart from the large air and army bases, there were numerous smaller installations where a few concrete or Nissen huts accommodated personnel for a searchlight battery, a radar station or a small training establishment. Reservoirs were built as precautions against air raids. In Ludlow one stood in Castle Square and another in the moat of the castle. The Shrewsbury and Church Stretton by-passes were used as marshalling areas for military vehicles in the period prior to D-Day, and many remained long after VE Day. Wide roadside verges were filled with dumps of ammunition which remained around Craven Arms and Ludlow for many months after the war ended.

159 *A hangar and Nissen huts at Peplow airfield.*

Only eight lives were lost in the county in air raids, but the rivers Teme and Severn provided landmarks for German bombers bound for Merseyside, and many bombs were jettisoned by raiders anxious to return home. Two people were killed on 29 August 1940 in Church Street, Bridgnorth, where the site of the bombed house is marked by a garden of remembrance. There were three further fatalities in Ellesmere Road, Shrewsbury, two days later, but many bombs fell harmlessly in rural areas. Huge craters were made between Caer Caradoc and Little Caradoc on 22 October 1940 and on Lilleshall golf course on 28 September. A haystack was destroyed at Woore, and some windows broken in Tugford. A spectacular raid was directed at the southern end of the Stiperstones on the night of 9-10 April 1941. It went unreported, perhaps because it was the result of a British intelligence operation designed to confuse the Luftwaffe, but the headmistress of the Bog School recorded that the first group of German planes circled overhead dropping flares. They were followed by a second wave bringing hundreds of incendiary bombs, which failed to cause substantial fires on the rain-sodden hillsides. A third wave of bombers brought high explosive bombs which rained over the area between the Devil's Chair and the Bog without causing significant damage. Even one which fell at the entrance to the playground of the Bog School failed to break a single pane of glass. Only one V1 Flying Bomb, which came down at Tong on Christmas Eve 1944, reached the county.

Salopians were urged to keep rabbits, to save fuel, to contribute money to National Savings in events like Wings for Victory weeks, and to join the Home Guard. The comedian George Robey took the salute during a 'War-ship Week' parade in Shifnal. The Women's Institutes opened a stall in Oswestry market in June 1940 for the sale of produce, and in 1943 the Shropshire institutes made 92,642 lbs. of jam, more than any other county in the W.I. national scheme. Four American-built 2-8-0 locomotives began to work from Shrewsbury in January 1942, but they and some later arrivals of the same type had all departed for service in continental Europe by September 1944. A night canteen and hostel for travelling and stranded servicemen was opened at 4 Chester Street, Shrewsbury on 20 December 1939, and operated throughout the war. Country houses were turned over to new purposes. When James Lees-Milne visited Attingham on behalf of

160 *The first seven officers of 'F' (Ludlow) Company of the Home Guard assembled at Ludlow Castle (SO50-8745) during the Second World War. Back row: Lieut. R. Akroyd, Lieut. (later Capt.) C.E. Lloyd, Lieut. (later Major) G.T. Bennett, Lieut. W.J. Beniams. Front row: Capt. A.W. Churchill, Lieut.-Col. G. Windsor-Clive, C.M.G., M.P., Lieut. (later Capt.) A.L. Crow.*

the National Trust on 7-8 June 1943 he found that most of the house was occupied by WAAFs, with the fireplaces and dadoes boarded up, but that, in the few rooms which remained to him in the east wing, Lord Berwick was still able to express his worries about ghosts, one of which he thought to have disguised itself as a vacuum cleaner.

From 1942 American and Canadian servicemen were stationed in Shropshire, and for their benefit a Red Cross Leave Club was established at the *Raven Hotel* in Shrewsbury from 1 May 1943. American troops took part in the 'Salute the Soldier' week in Ludlow in May 1944, and the USAF flew Lockheed Lightnings from Atcham and Air Cobras from High Ercall.

The Shropshire press during the last 18 months of the European war reflects something of the atmosphere conveyed in Humphrey Jennings's film *Diary for Timothy*, made in the winter of 1944-45, which subtly mixes images of the closing phases of the war, the newly-born child of an officer serving overseas, a miner injured at his work, an engine driver, Dame Myra Hess playing Beethoven in the National Gallery, a constant scurrying about the streets of small groups of uniformed figures. Jennings poses questions about the direction which society would take when the war was over. There was in Shropshire a willingness to try new experiences. In January 1944 Sir John Barbirolli gave a series of concerts, including Mozart's 40th Symphony, Beethoven's 5th and Tchaikovsky's 4th at the Granada cinema in Shrewsbury. In a town hard pressed by the billeting authorities people gladly made room in their homes for the musicians. Barbirolli spoke of the 'sudden desire all over the country to hear music'. Moiseiwitch gave piano recitals in the town in February and Clifford Curzon in March.

Equally unusual was an American football match played between two service teams at the Gay Meadow in November 1944. Salopians strove to understand P.A.Y.E., and discussed the need for sex education, which had been highlighted by the use of market towns as recreational centres for troops. There was much discussion of the 1944 Education Act. The building of new houses for agricultural workers in places like Plealey Road had already commenced.

VE Day, 8 May 1945 was celebrated with gusto. In Shrewsbury the borough council fitted up an old gramophone on the Market Hall to provide music for dancing. At Much Wenlock an effigy of Hitler was burned on Windmill Hill, while a comic football match took place on the Olympian Field. The news of victory over Japan was first heard in Shrewsbury at the American Red Cross Club late in the evening of 15 August. Soldiers rushed into the street to light a bonfire, and were joined by A.T.S. girls in their pyjamas. The following day flags and bunting were flying in Mardol by noon, and in the evening policemen could be seen dancing with Land Girls in the Square and a man asking for a hat for Lord Clive from the top of the statue was handed 'a pair of lovely silk cami-knickers'. Many features of wartime Shropshire were on the point of disappearance. The county civil defence organisation held its farewell parade on the playing fields of Shrewsbury School. Parts of the Sentinel Works had been adapted to make steel kitchen and bathroom units for prefabs at a rate of 320 per week, and German prisoners of war were laying sewers on the new council estate at Crowmoor, Shrewsbury. A Labour Party candidate, Ivor Thomas, won the Wrekin constituency contest with a major of over 5,000 in the general election.

In Shropshire, as elsewhere, people expected that the sacrifices of wartime would bring a better life and that wartime comradeship would be extended, sentiments expressed with eloquence in a letter to a local newspaper by an aircraftman from St George's writing from the Middle East in 1944. The National Health Service took over the county's hospitals; its coal mines, railways and gas and electricity undertakings were nationalised, and there was a massive programme of rural electrification. By the beginning of 1946 Shrewsbury Borough Council had still to complete a new house, but the first two new private dwellings in the town were hailed in the press. By the following August, 57 out of a projected 100 'prefabs' at Crowmoor were occupied, but a start on 100 permanent homes on an adjacent site was delayed by a shortage of bricks. In September it was reported that local authorities in the county had built 166 prefabs and 22 permanent houses, but that 137 prefabs and 781 permanent dwellings were under construction. Among the houses constructed during this period were those at Arleston Lane at Wellington and Dodmore Lane at Ludlow, and an estate of 70 houses and eight flats at Callow Hill, Minsterley.

Impatience with the slowness of the building programme and the overcrowded conditions in which many ex-servicemen were living led many homeless families to occupy ex-Army and ex-R.A.F. camps and houses vacated by the military during the summer of 1946. Some houses in Baldwin

161 *The school at Church Preen, one of the first village primary schools to be built in the post-war period.*

Webb Avenue, Donnington, which had been left empty after military families had moved out, were occupied, and the remaining empty dwellings in the road were guarded by troops. Patrols with fixed bayonets protected the former army camp at Apley Castle, Wellington. Squatters moved into concrete huts at Leaton where the A.T.S. had operated a bakery, while other groups occupied a military camp at Arleston, a former Italian prisoner-of-war camp at St George's and the air base at Atcham.

In the first week of January 1944 the Shropshire Education Committee welcomed R.A. Butler's Education Act, Sir Offley Wakeman commenting that it was:

> a very far reaching measure ... it gives new opportunities to the great mass of children of this country such as they never had before ... I hope that this committee and the council will make facilities for the education of its children and young people in Shropshire as great as those of any county in the kingdom.

Sir Offley, who was chairman of the Education Committee from 1944-67, and his chief officer, H. Martin Wilson, transformed the education system in the county into one which by the time of Wilson's retirement in 1965 had an international reputation. Many new primary school buildings were constructed and the county became celebrated for its progressive primary teaching methods. After 1954 secondary school construction commenced and in 1965 the last of the 207 all-age schools which had existed in 1945 ceased to teach children over the age of eleven. A Farm Institute was established at Walford, a residential adult college at Attingham Park (closed in 1975) and several innovative special schools were opened. This was achieved in the face of much opposition from a traditionally-minded county council many of whose members were committed to minimum levels of public expenditure. Wilson commented that in the 1940s the Education Committee was 'something more like an anti-education committee'.

The first post-war West Midland Show was held in 1946 and was intended as an unambitious one-day event, a homely gathering of the agricultural community. Over 30,000 people attended and there was traffic chaos. The Agriculture Act of the following year, largely based on wartime experience, brought a new prosperity to agriculture. In 1951 Lilleshall Hall became a residential sports centre with the aid of the South African Aid to Britain Fund. League football came to Shropshire when Shrewsbury Town F.C. was elected to the Football League in 1950. The first Ludlow Festival was held in 1953. Traditional industries continued to decline. There were 16 mines in the Coalbrookdale coalfield at the time of nationalisation in 1947 but only three by 1963. The smelting of iron in Shropshire ceased when the Lilleshall Company's blast furnaces at Priorslee were blown out in 1959. In Shrewsbury the Sentinel Waggon Works built its last steam waggons in 1949, constructed 1,350 oil-engined lorries and buses between 1946 and 1956, and was then acquired by Rolls Royce Ltd. which transferred its oil engine division to the factory in 1959. New industries like the making of swim suits in Shrewsbury flourished. Shropshire's largest employer, G.K.N. Sankey at Hadley, shared the successes of the British motor industry of the period, and drew in labour from almost every corner of the county.

20

The Last Thirty Years 1963-93

The mid-1960s were years of optimism in Shropshire as in the nation at large. The English football team trained at Lilleshall Hall before winning the World Cup in 1966. The new Shirehall in Abbey Foregate, Shrewsbury was opened in 1966. The 9.5 acre (3.8 ha.) site was acquired in stages between 1945 and 1965. Ground preparation began in 1963, and construction commenced in 1964. The Ironbridge B power station with two 500 MW turbine generators, costing £50,000,000 and employing 540 staff, began to operate in 1969, its 670ft. (204m.) chimney and four cooling towers becoming landmarks visible from all over the county. In Shrewsbury the county's first large supermarket opened with balloons and bunting in 1964. The county's evening newspaper, the *Shropshire Star*, was successfully launched on 5 October 1964, a day when dense fog covered the West Midlands.

The most momentous expression of this optimism was the designation of a new town in the Coalbrookdale Coalfield in January 1963. The West Midlands conurbation was then a thriving industrial region. It was believed that the population at large would continue to increase rapidly, and that it was desirable to relieve congestion by moving people from Birmingham and Wolverhampton to new and expanded towns. There was an obviously practical argument for using for building land laid waste by the Industrial Revolution rather than prime agricultural land, and the conversion of the derelict landscape of the coalfield into a city for the 21st century seemed in the 1960s a noble and Romantic quest.

162 *Shrewsbury's 20th-century market hall, which replaced the Victorian market hall of 1869 in the mid-1960s (SJ490125).*

163 *The Ironbridge Gorge from Leighton Bank (SJ617050) showing on the left the Ironbridge A power station, built in 1932 and demolished in 1983, and on the right the cooling towers of the Ironbridge B station, completed in the late 1960s.*

A journalist, A.W. Bowdler, first publicly suggested that a new town might be created in the coalfield in the *Birmingham Gazette* on 16 February 1955 and by the end of the year the County Council was discussing with Birmingham City Council an overspill scheme to accommodate 10,000 people in Dawley, and the prospects of developing a satellite town of 100,000 people. In 1960 the Minister of Housing and Local Government announced that Dawley was being considered as the site for a new town, and the following year A.G. Sheppard Fidler, city architect of Birmingham, was asked to examine the prospects. He reported in February 1962, and in January 1963 the new town was designated under the New Towns Act of 1946 and its development corporation appointed. The town comprised that part of the coalfield between the A5 and the Severn, and was named Dawley. In 1964 the Corporation set up its headquarters at Priorslee Hall. John H.D. Madin & Partners were commissioned as planning consultants in September 1963 and published their draft master plan in January 1965. The following July the Minister of Housing, Richard Crossman, ordered that an overall plan for the coalfield should be prepared. Madin's proposals entitled *Dawley: Wellington: Oakengates* were published in 1966, and in December 1968 Anthony Greenwood, by then Minister of Housing, confirmed an order designating as a new town the whole of the coalfield north of the Severn with a narrow strip on the south bank of the river through the Ironbridge Gorge. The minister personally named it Telford.

Meanwhile the Development Corporation had begun to transform the landscape of the southern part of the area. The canal basin at Tweedale became an industrial estate where the first factory was handed over in September 1966. The first housing estate was built at Sutton Hill where site preparation began in March 1966 and the first house was occupied in March 1967. A by-pass around the centre of Madeley was completed in March 1969. Through the 1970s building work on a vast scale could be observed between the A5 and the Severn: housing developments like

Brookside and Hollinswood; traffic-free shopping centres at Dawley and Oakengates; industrial estates at Halesfield and Stafford Park and the restoration of historic buildings in Priorslee village and the Ironbridge Gorge. The mains drainage arrangements in the region were chaotic, and an essential preliminary to large-scale re-development was the building of new systems with treatment works at Gitchfield in the south and Rushmoor in the north. The road system was similarly deficient and has been transformed by the building of stretches of dual carriageway and by-passes around shopping centres. Approximately 5,000 acres (2,020 ha.) of the designated area were termed derelict, of which by the mid-1980s some 4,000 (1,616 ha.) were reclaimed. The most dramatic of the reclamation schemes was undertaken in the mid-1970s on the site of the former Old Park Ironworks and its surrounding collieries.

In October 1973 when the first shops in the new centre of Telford were opened, the Yom Kippur war was being fought in the Middle East and was followed by the oil embargo and a massive rise in oil prices which induced a severe recession. Optimism turned to pessimism, which was reinforced as far as Telford was concerned by a rethinking of regional strategy. By 1971 it was recognised that the population predictions of the 1960s were exaggerated, and that the removal of industry from the Birmingham conurbation might be detrimental to that area's prosperity. In September 1976 Peter Shore, Minister of Housing, revealed that future government policy would be to transfer investment from new towns to inner-city areas. The population of Telford, which had been predicted in 1965 to rise to over 220,000 by 1990, was revised to one of 135,000 by 1986, rising to 150,000 in the following decade. The growth of the town had been hampered by several factors. In its early years the areas from which it could draw industry were circumscribed. Telford proved a fertile seedbed for new industrial ventures, but it never received the boost which it had been anticipated would come from the establishment of a large concern. The new town was isolated from the Inter City railway network and from the motorway system. It also suffered from the decline of some of the area's established industries. The disappearance of the basic industries of the Industrial Revolution was predictable. Both the major collieries working when the new town was designated have closed, the closure of Granville in 1979 marking the end of deep mining in the Shropshire coalfield. Several brick and tile works and much of the railway system have similarly closed. What was not anticipated in the 1960s was the demise of many factories which then seemed securely established. G.K.N. Sankey, which was employing about 7,500 people in 1965 was employing less than 3,000 by the early 1980s. Like all new towns, Telford suffered from spells of disillusion. One nadir was reached in January 1974 when a local newspaper published a feature on the Woodside housing area entitled 'Sin City'.

The fortunes of Telford changed in the mid-1980s. On 23 November 1983 the section of the M54 motorway between the M6 and Telford was opened, to be followed in 1987 by the completion of Telford Central railway station which until 1992 was served by regular Inter City trains from

164 *Three Ironbridge logos.*

London. It was also in 1983 that Maxell became the first Japanese company to set up a factory in Telford. By the middle of 1991 there were 22 Japanese firms in the town. Industry grew rapidly in the 1980s, due partly to the designation of an Enterprise Zone in which 7,000 new jobs were created. Telford Development Corporation ceased to exist in September 1991. Over a period of 28 years it had been responsible for the transformation of the Coalbrookdale coalfield. It is too early to judge the long-term success of the Corporation. Several aspects of the town, the Radburn layouts at Sutton Hill and Woodside, and the shopping precinct at Madeley, are monuments to discarded planning assumptions. Social problems remain even in some of the newly-built parts of the town. Nevertheless there is a measure of prosperity in the Shropshire Coalfield arising from a manufacturing and service economy of a kind which was scarcely imaginable in the mid-1960s.

The birth of Telford is the most spectacular aspect of the process of de-industrialisation which has characterised Shropshire during the last century, and the first instance in which government investment has been applied in an attempt to solve the social problems which arise from the decline of mines and manufactures. In earlier decades the response to the closure of industrial concerns in the Coalbrookdale Coalfield was emigration to other parts of England, and the growth of a culture of unemployment, of which poaching formed a significant part, amongst some of those who remained. In other areas, like the coalfield around Oswestry, mining communities have become commuter villages while pitheads have been adapted to small-scale industrial uses. A similar process has occurred at Highley and Alveley in the Wyre Forest Coalfield, while in the lead-mining region around the Stiperstones squatter cottages amongst the waste tips have become the residences of commuters and artists.

165 *One of the best-restored railway landscapes in Britain, the station at Highley on the Severn Valley Railway (SO749830).*

Salop County Council was one of the few authorities to undertake its responsibilities under the 1958 Local Government, and the only one to complete a thoroughgoing reorganisation of district council boundaries. Many of the small district councils in Shropshire were amalgamated in 1966, but this pattern of organisation was short-lived, for the 1972 Local Government Act, implemented in 1974, reduced the number of districts to six. The area governed by the County Council remained unchanged by the 1972 Act, but the abolition of the office of alderman led to changes in the personnel and outlook of the council. The official name of the county authority was changed from Salop County Council to Shropshire County Council in 1980.

In 1974 the Ministry of Transport began to make resources available for the improvement of roads and the County Council adopted a 10-year programme for major routes. From 1967 a further programme for trunk roads commenced and since that time substantial changes have been made, particularly on the A49, the A53, the A458 and the A442. During the 1980s by-passes were constructed for Shrewsbury, Ludlow, Oswestry, Bridgnorth, Prees and Newport. The Beeching Plan led to the closure of the Severn Valley Railway, the Much Wenlock branch, the Wellington-Crewe and Stafford lines, and the whole of the Cambrian Railways main line from Buttington to Whitchurch with the exception of a siding serving the Blodwell Rocks quarries. The running sheds, goods yards and locomotive works at Oswestry were closed. In 1967 the main railway between Euston, the West Midlands and the North West was electrified. Trains from Shrewsbury ceased to run to Wolverhampton Low Level, Birmingham Snow Hill and London Paddington, but went instead to Wolverhampton High Level, Birmingham New Street and London Euston. Through trains from

166 Passenger trains returned to Coalbrook-dale (SJ667048) on Sundays during the summer of 1979, and again in 1988-90. In this picture the inaugural train of the 1988 season passes the Old Furnace on 13 June 1988.

167 *The most spectacular way to leave Shropshire: Thomas Telford's aqueduct of 1801 carrying the Ellesmere Canal and Henry Robertson's viaduct of 1848 carrying the Shrewsbury & Chester Railway across the Ceiriog from Shropshire into Denbighshire (SJ287373).*

Lancashire to the West of England ceased to run through Shrewsbury and Ludlow in 1969. Services on the route changed every few years during the 1970s and '80s, but ultra-modern rolling stock now provides an hourly service between Manchester and Cardiff.

Attitudes to the Shropshire landscape and to its past have changed considerably over the last 30 years. In 1974 the County Council established a Museums Service, the main activity of which has been the development of a farm museum at Acton Scott which opened in 1975. Many urban areas have been designated 'conservation areas' under the Civic Amenities Act of 1967. The Shrewsbury Civic Society took an important lead in undertaking the restoration of Bear Steps, a range of 15th-century buildings in the town centre, which was completed in 1972. The restoration set a pattern for the adaptive re-use of historic buildings in Shrewsbury, and marked the reversal of a tendency which had lasted for many decades to destroy such buildings. The last two decades have seen the restoration of some of the town's most splendid timber-framed structures, among them Barracks Passage, Riggs Hall and the *King's Head* in Mardol. New and profitable uses have been found for other buildings: St Julian's Church which is a craft centre, the Buttermarket in Howard Street which is a night club, and the Royal Salop Infirmary which has been divided into flats and small shops. The County Council was responsible for the restoration of Shrewsbury's library in Castle Gates, the original buildings of Shrewsbury School.

Local history and archaeology societies have been established in many parts of the county, and have produced trail guides, published books of old photographs and organised programmes of guided walks which have increased popular interest in the county's history. A group has embarked on an ambitious programme of research which should make Ludlow one of the best understood as well as the most beautiful of historic towns.

On the county's western border the W.E.A. and the Y.H.A. began to arrange walks along Offa's Dyke in 1961, most of them led by the late Frank Noble, the local W.E.A. organiser. Interest in the dyke had been stimulated by surveys each summer between 1925 and 1932 and subsequent publications by Sir Cyril Fox. A path along the Dyke had been designated in 1955, but it had remained a legal rather than a practical concept. After the designation of the Countryside Commission in 1968, it was possible to pursue the project with more energy. New rights were negotiated, signposts erected and stiles constructed, and on 10 July 1971 the Offa's Dyke Path was declared open by Lord Hunt of Llanvair Waterdine, leader of the team which in 1953 made the first ascent of Mount Everest.

Two major developments in transport conservation have taken place in Shropshire. In 1954 the Llangollen line of the Ellesmere Canal was almost closed, but was retained as a means of supplying water to the towns of mid-Cheshire. It became, with the main line of the Shropshire Union, one of the most popular stretches of water for canal holidays. Holiday cruising on the canal had begun as early as 1934 when the vessel *Seamew* could be hired from Ellesmere. Two years after the closure of the Severn Valley Railway, a meeting was called in Kidderminster in July 1965 to consider the formation of a preservation society. In May 1967 a new company was formed to operate the route, which now provides services through from Bridgnorth to Kidderminster, and is one of the most successful preserved railways in Britain.

Changes in attitudes to the past have also come in the Ironbridge Gorge. In his account of Shropshire written in 1912, which mirrored the popular wisdom of the time, the Rev. J.E. Auden described Ironbridge as 'an uninteresting and somewhat squalid town'. The following year Ironbridge impressed J.J. Hissey to ask who but the Devil 'could have entered into the mind of man to cause him to spoil so fare [*sic*] a spot for the sake of mere money-making?'. He considered Ironbridge to be 'dirty, mean and ugly ... squalid and smoky', and saw no beauty in the Iron Bridge. Few Salopians regarded the coalfield as one of the jewels of the county in the 1950s, but

168 *Distinguished Belgian visitors to Ironbridge; M. Paul Lohest (right) who designed the Ronquières inclined plane of the 1960s and M. Maurice Kemouchamps who has designed the vertical lift at Strépy Thieu, stand at the top of the Hay Inclined Plane in the Blists Hill Open Air Museum on 18 April 1984 (SJ694025).*

169 *The Iron Bridge (SJ672034) showing the woodworking techniques by which the iron ribs were held together.*

in 1955 the late Michael Rix praised its beauty in an article in which the term 'industrial archaeology' first appeared in print. In 1959, in commemoration of the 250th anniversary of the invention of coke smelting, Allied Ironfounders Ltd. uncovered the Old Furnace at Coalbrookdale, and set up a small museum alongside it. The Telford Development Corporation took the initiative in setting up the Ironbridge Gorge Museum Trust in 1967. The Trust absorbed the Coalbrookdale Museum in 1970. It appointed its first staff in 1969 and its first director in 1971. In its early years it received enthusiastic volunteer support. In 1973 the Blists Hill Open Air Museum was formally opened to the public and work began on the restoration of the Iron Bridge. A museum was set up in the Coalport Chinaworks in 1976. The following year a visitor centre was opened in the curious Gothic warehouse which the Coalbrookdale Company had built beside the Severn. In 1979 a new Museum of Iron, replacing that established in 1959, was opened in the Great Warehouse at Coalbrookdale. The restoration of the Iron Bridge was completed in 1980. In 1982 a cover building protecting the Old Furnace in Coalbrookdale was finished, and the Museum's library was moved to the nearby Long Warehouse, which since 1984 has also housed the Ironbridge Institute. The Museum won the Museum of the Year Award in 1977 and the European Museum of the Year Award in the following year, amongst other commendations, and has helped to transform the economy of the Gorge, which in 1986 became a UNESCO World Heritage Site.

The history of Shropshire over the last three decades shows the futility of prediction, but it is a reasonable assumption that Shropshire's history will be more of a reality to future than to past generations. Offa's Dyke, Ludlow and Ironbridge are historical treasures of exceptional value, and the recognition of their significance within the last 30 years should prove of lasting benefit.

Select Bibliography

Standard Works of Reference

The books listed below are fundamental to any serious study of the history of Shropshire, but since they are scarce or expensive most readers will need to seek them in libraries.

Burn, Charlotte, *Shropshire Folk Lore* (1883/86)
Cranage, D.H.S., *An Architectural Account of the Churches of Shropshire* (1894-1912)
Eyton, R.W., *The Antiquities of Shropshire* (1854-60)
Owen, H. and Blakeway, J.B., *A History of Shrewsbury* (1825)
Transactions of the Shropshire Archaeological Society
The Victoria History of the Counties of England: Shropshire, vol. I (1908), vol. II (1973), vol. III (1979), vol. IV (1989), vol. VIII (1968), vol. XI (1985)

Other Works

The list which follows is not a comprehensive bibliography of the county's history, but provides a range of books which take further some of the themes discussed in the chapters above. All the books on the list can be obtained reasonably easily, even if some are no longer in print.

Alfrey, J. & Clark, C.M., *Landscape of Industry: Patterns of change in the Ironbridge Gorge* (1993)
Barker, P. A., *From Roman Viroconium to Medieval Wroxeter* (1990)
Baugh, G.C. and Cox, D.C., *Monastic Shropshire* (1981)
Baugh, G.C. and Cox, D.C., *Shropshire and its Rulers* (1979)
Baxton, R., *The Autobiography of Richard Baxter*, ed. Keeble, N.H. (1974)
Beresford, M., *New Towns of the Middle Ages* (1968)
Bilbey, D., *Church Stretton* (1985)
Booth, T., *Watermills on the River Rea* (1990)
Brook, F. and Allbutt, M., *The Shropshire Lead Mines* (1973)
Brown, I.J., *The Mines of Shropshire* (1976)
Carr, A., *Shrewsbury: A Pictorial History* (1994)
Cartledge, J.E.G., *The Vale and Gates of Usc-Con* (1934, rep. 1982)
Carver, M.O.H., *Prehistory in Lowland Shropshire* (1991)
Cathrall, W., *The History of Oswestry* (1855, rep. 1974)
Champion, W., *Everyday Life in Tudor Shrewsbury* (1994)
Chitty, L.F., *Days on the Dyke* (1980)
Christiansen, R., *A Regional History of the Railways of Great Britain, VII, The West Midlands* (1974)
Clark, C.M., *Ironbridge Gorge* (1993)
Cossons, N. and Trinder, B., *The Iron Bridge* (1979)
Cromarty, Dorothy, *Everyday Life in Medieval Shrewsbury* (1991)
Cromarty, D. and Cromarty, R., *The Wealth of Shrewsbury in the early 14th century* (1993)
Darwin, C., *The Autobiography of Charles Darwin* (1929)
Davies, R.R., *Lordship and Society in the March of Wales, 1282-1400* (1978)
Desmond, A. and Moore, J., *Darwin* (1991)
Elliott, D.J., *Shropshire Clockmakers* (1979)
Evans, G. and Briscoe, R., *Telford: A Pictorial History* (1995)
Faraday, M., *Ludlow 1085-1660: A Social, Economic and Political History* (1991)

Farrow, W.J., *The Great Civil War in Shropshire* (1926)

Foulkes, F.W., *Hooked on Cheese* (1985)

Fox, Sir Cyril, *Offa's Dyke* (1955)

Foxall, H.D.G., *Shropshire Field Names* (1980)

Gale, W.K.V. and Nicholls, C.R., *The Lilleshall Company 1764-1964* (1979)

Garbett, S., *The History of Wem* (1818, rep. 1982)

Gelling, Margaret, *The Place Names of Shropshire* (1990)

Gladstone, E.W., *The Shropshire Yeomanry* (1953)

Gough, Richard, *The History of Myddle* (ed. David Hey, 1981)

Griffiths, Edward, *The Bishop's Castle Railway* (1977)

Hadfield, C., *The Canals of the West Midlands* (1966)

Harris, Donald F., *The Work of Canadian Emigration Agents in Shropshire, 1896-1914* (1991)

Hart, Sheila, *Shrewsbury: A Portrait in Old Picture Postcards* (1988)

Hey, David, *An English Rural Community: Myddle under the Tudors and Stuarts* (1974)

Hill, M.C., *The Demesne and the Waste: a study of medieval inclosure on the manor of High Ercall 1086-1399* (1984)

Hinton, J.V., *Wheathill 1086 to 1986* (1986)

Hollins, A., *The Farmer, the Plough and the Devil: The Story of Fordhall Farm, Pioneer of Organic Farming* (1986)

Hughes, W.J. and Thomas, J.L., *'The Sentinel': a history of Alley & MacLellan and The Sentinel Waggon Works, I, 1875-1930* (1973); *see also* Thomas, J.L.

Hunt, Dame Agnes, *This is My Life* (1938)

Jarvis, M., *Captain Webb and 100 years of Channel Swimming* (1975)

Klingender, F., *Art and the Industrial Revolution* (1947)

Lawford, J.P., *Clive: Proconsul of India* (1976)

Leach, C., *A School at Shrewsbury* (1990)

Lead, P., *Agents of Revolution: John and Thomas Gilbert—Entrepreneurs* (1989)

Lewis, C.P. and Thorn, F.R., *The Shropshire Domesday* (1990)

Lloyd, D., *Broad Street* [Ludlow]: *its houses and their residents* (1979)

Lloyd, D., *County Grammar School: a history of Ludlow Grammar School* (1977)

Lloyd, D., *Ludlow* (1995)

Lloyd, D. and Klein, P., *Ludlow: A Historic Town in Words and Pictures* (1984)

Lloyd, D. and Moran, M., *The Corner Shop* (1978)

Lloyd, J.E., *A History of Wales* (1911)

Lynch, F. and Burgess, C., *Prehistoric Man in Wales and the West* (1972)

Madin, J.H.D. and Partners, *Dawley: Wellington: Oakengates* (1966)

McInnes, A., *The English Town 1660-1760* (1980)

Merry, D.T., *The History of Minsterley* (1976)

Milne, James Lees, *Ancestral Voices* (1975)

Morris, John, *Domesday Book: Staffordshire* (1976)

Morriss, R.K., *Rail Centres: Shrewsbury* (1986)

Morriss, R.K., *The Canals of Shropshire* (1991)

Moulsdale, J.P., *The King's Shropshire Light Infantry* (1972)

Mumford, W.F., *Wenlock in the Middle Ages* (1977)

Muter, W.G., *The Buildings of an Industrial Community, Coalbrookdale and Ironbridge* (1979)

Nair, Gwyneth, *Highley: the development of a Community 1550-1880* (1988)

Namier, L.B., *The Structure of Politics at the Accession of George III* (1928, rep. 1957)

Noble, Frank, *Offa's Dyke Path* (1969)

Owen, Harold, *Journey from Obscurity* (1963)

Owen, Hugh, *Some Account of the Ancient and Present State of Shrewsbury* (1808, rep. 1972)

Penfold, Alastair, *Thomas Telford: Engineer* (1980)

Pevsner, N., *The Buildings of England: Shropshire* (1980)

Philpott, B.M., *A Name, A Man, A House: Oakley Manor, Shrewsbury* (1983)

Pidgeon, Henry, *Memorials of Shrewsbury* (1837, rep. 1975)

Powell, J. and Vanns, M.A., *South Telford: Ironbridge Gorge, Madeley and Dawley* (1995)

Powell, J. and Vanns, M.A., *North Telford: Wellington, Oakengates and Surrounding Areas* (1995)

Prentice, R., *A History of Newport* (1986)

Preshous, Janet, *Bishop's Castle Well-Remembered* (1990)

Raistrick, Arthur, *Dynasty of Ironfounders* (1953, rep. 1989)

Randall, J., *The History of Madeley* (1880, rep. 1975)

Rayska, S., *Victorian and Edwardian Shropshire from old photographs* (1977)

Reeves, F., *Ludlow in Wartime* (1981)

Richards, E., *The Leviathan of Wealth* (1973)

Rimmer, W.G., *Marshalls of Leeds: Flax Spinners 1781-1886* (1960)

Robinson, D.H., *The Sleepy Meese* (1988)

Rolt, L.T.C., *Thomas Telford* (1958)

Rolt, L.T.C., *Landscape with Canals* (1977)

Rowley, N. and S.V., *Market Drayton: a study in Social History* (1966)

Rowley, Trevor, *The Shropshire Landscape* (1972)

Ruckley, H., *Oswestry Racecourse* (1989)

Russell, R., *Lost Canals of England and Wales* (1971, rep. 1982)

Seaby, W.A. and Smith, A.C., *Windmills in Shropshire Hereford and Worcester: a contemporary survey* (1984)

Sherwood, R.E., *Civil Strife in the Midlands 1642-51* (1974)

Slack, W.J., *The Lordship of Oswestry* (1951)

Speight, M., *The Great Houses* (1980)

Speight, M. and Lloyd, D., *Ludlow Houses and their Residents* (1978)

Smith, D.J., *The Severn Valley Railway* (1968)

Smith, D.J., *Action Stations: Military Airfields of Wales and the North West* (1981)

Smith, S.B., *A View from the Iron Bridge* (1979)

Smith, W. and Beddoes, K., *The Cleobury Mortimer and Ditton Priors Light Railway* (1980)

De Soissons, M., *Telford: the Making of Shropshire's New Town* (1991)

Stallworthy, Jon, *Wilfred Owen* (1974)

Stamper, Paul, *'The Farmer Feeds Us All': a Short History of Shropshire Agriculture* (1989)

Stamper, Paul, *Historic Parks and Gardens of Shropshire* (1996)

Stanford, S.C., *Archaeology in the Welsh Marches* (1980)

Stratton, M.J., *Ironbridge and Electric Revolution* (1994)

Thomas, A.R. and J.L., *'The Sentinel': a history of Alley & MacLellan and The Sentinel Waggon Works, II, 1930-1980* (1987); *see also* Hughes, W.J.

Thomas, R.D., *Industries of the Morda Valley* (1939, rep. 1978)

Thorn, F. and C., *Domesday Book: Shropshire* (1986)

Thornburn, E., *First into Antwerp: the part played by the 4th Battalion K.S.L.I. in the Liberation of the City in September 1974* (1987)

Tonks, E.S., *The Shropshire and Montgomeryshire Railway* (1972)

Tonks, E.S., *The Snailbeach District Railways* (1974)

Trinder, Barrie, *The Industrial Archaeology of Shropshire* (1996)

Trinder, Barrie, *The Industrial Revolution in Shropshire* (1973, rep.1981)

Trinder, Barrie, *The Darbys of Coalbrookdale* (1974, rep. 1978, 1981, 1991)

Trinder, Barrie, *Victorian Shrewsbury* (1984)

Trinder, Barrie and Cox, Jeff, *Yeomen and Colliers in Telford* (1980)

Trumper, D., *Shrewsbury in Old Photographs* (1994)

Trumper, D., *Shrewsbury: A Second Selection* (1995)

Wacher, J., *The Towns of Roman Britain* (1974)

Watkin, I., *Oswestry, with an account of its old houses &c* (1920, rep. 1982)

Watts, Sylvia, *Shifnal: a Pictorial History* (1989)

Williams, D., *A History of Modern Wales* (1950)

Williams, Penry, *The Council in the Marches of Wales under Elizabeth I* (1958)

Webster, Graham, *The Cornovii* (1975, rep. 1991)

Wilson, Edward, *The Ellesmere and Llangollen Canal* (1975)

Wilson, Martin, *Epoch in English Education: Administrator's Challenge* (1985)

Wright, Thomas, *The History and Antiquities of Ludlow* (1826, rep. 1972)

Index